A Door of Hope

My Search for the
Treasures of the Copper Scroll

A Door of Hope

My Search for the Treasures of the Copper Scroll

by
Vendyl Jones

LIGHTCATCHER BOOKS
Springdale, Arkansas

Editor, Jim Long
Cover design and layout by Carol Long
Author photo by Jim Long
Photos, except where noted, are from Lightcatcher Productions

A Door of Hope

My Search for the Treasures of the Copper Scroll

ISBN 0-9719388-5-7

10 9 8 7 6 5 4 3 2 1

Printed in the United States of America on acid-free paper. For information write to Lightcatcher Books, 842 Kissinger Ave., Springdale AR 72762, or visit our website: www.lightcatcherbooks.com

"And I will give her vineyards from there, and the valley of Achor for a door of hope; and she shall sing there, as in the days of her youth, and as in the day when she came out of the land of Egypt."

— *Hosea 2:17*

Table of Contents

Acknowledgments

If you find any joy, enlightenment or entertainment value in these pages then we both can thank a number of friends beginning with the G-d of Israel, He is One and His Name is One.

I would like to thank the following for their support, encouragement, cajoling and loving threats. I appreciate Jim Long, my editor and publisher at Lightcatcher Books, for asking me to tell my story. His ability to comprehend my particular brand of Vendyl-speak has guided this book from conception, birth and delivery. The layout and book cover design reflect the good taste of Jim's wife and partner, Carol Long, of Lightcatcher Books. Thanks to Gerald Robins for lending us his incredible eye for detail. He labored over the proofing while offering sound editorial advice. Adam Penrod gets pat on the back for his unfailing assistance, and for keeping the lines of communication open between all parties as the book was being written. Much appreciation goes to Don Hutchison who continues to support all of my efforts and keeps me on my toes by asking the right questions.

My wonderfully faithful supporters are a big reason that I am allowed to continue. I am indebted to each and every one of you for your continual faith in our mission. If you don't find your name in this book, please know that there are so many of you that we could fill the pages of another book. Finally, I dedicate this book to my loving wife, Anita Shay Jones. She is, indeed, a woman of valor.

Vendyl M. Jones
Grand Prairie, Texas
2005/ 5765

Acknowledgements

Publisher's Preface

Before I accompanied Professor Vendyl Jones on my first archaeological dig in Israel, I was a student in his Torah classes in Arlington, Texas. One of the first things Vendyl taught me was the twenty-two letters of the Hebrew *aleph-beit*. That simple act would be my first step in an ongoing journey of discovery as the riches of the Torah were opened up to me. I learned that Hebrew is read from right to left and that the modifier comes after the noun it modifies. For instance, *Shlomo Ha Melekh*, literally translated, is read "Solomon the King".

This system of reading reveals profound meaning as one gets deeper into the study of Torah and history of the Jewish people. At first blush it appears that the Jews have it backward, especially if one agrees with academicians who ascribe Jewish history or beliefs as having been borrowed from "older" cultures.

Scholars tell us that the account of a global flood in the Book of Genesis was borrowed from the Gilgamesh epic. Still others would have us believe that the God of the Bible rubbed off on the Jewish people from their Canaanite neighbors. I mention all of this because it was the same thinking that caused intelligent scholars to dismiss the text of the Copper Scroll as a collection of folklore. The early Dead Sea Scroll editors sought to reinforce this view by presenting as evidence a set of Marble Tablets found locked in a vault in Beirut, Lebanon.

The text on the tablets, carved in graceful Hebrew characters, was an exciting forgotten Midrash recorded by the Jewish sages that revealed how the sacred wealth of Solomon's Temple was hidden by the Prophet Jeremiah and the Levites.

In an academic slap across the face of their Jewish contemporaries, the early Dead Sea Scroll editors declared the inscribed Midrash a legend, thus diminishing the value of any Midrash and consigning all to the realm of Mother Goose. Since the Marble Tablets tell us that Jeremiah's compatriots copied the same list of treasures and their depositories onto a Copper Scroll, it followed that this unique metallic document also contained nothing but myth.

But they got it backwards.

Today, no serious scholar believes that the list of treasures on the Copper Scroll is legend. A simple reading, without prejudice, will dispel that notion. It does not meet any of the criteria for folklore. There is no cast of heroes and villains—not even a plot. The style and content of the Copper Scroll is that of a list of goods and where they are hidden. The treasures listed are indeed fabulous— but the text is a still a simple inventory.

Since the Copper Scroll is genuine in every regard, it follows that the text of Marble Tablets is just as genuine. The words found on those tablets tell of fabulous sacred vessels from Solomon's Temple, including the lost Ark of the Covenant. Vendyl Jones always knew the text of the Copper Scroll was very real. His reasons are found in the covers of this book. Maybe it was his early schooling in Hebrew, reading from the opposite end of the page that taught him to think in opposition of the academicians. Possibly it was his sincere regard for the words of the Jewish sages. I suspect it was both.

Those of you acquainted with Professor Jones, know that he has lived an extraordinary life. Vendyl survived a high school lab explosion, got his field training while excavating burial mounds in the dusty Texas plains, and dodged bullets fired at him by the KKK. We hope you won't be disappointed but we wanted Vendyl to save those colorful and fascinating accounts for his autobiography. In the meantime, we have asked him to tell us why and where he began his quest for the Treasures of the Copper Scroll. This edition is in English so you will have to read from left to right.

Jim Long
Lightcatcher Books
5765/2005

Part One

The Past Beckons

The Hand That Rocks the Cradle

"Imagination is an almost divine faculty which, without recourse to any philosophical method, immediately perceives everything: the secret and intimate connections between things, correspondences and analogies."
— Charles Baudelaire

My father was a barber. He ran a little shop along a dusty main street in Sudan, Texas. My mother was his able business partner as the shop's beautician. One day she told dad that she couldn't look at another head of hair because she was sick. My mother went to see the doctor.

She said, "Dr. Foot you've got to give me something for this stomachache."

He replied, "Vera, I'll give you seven or eight months — you're pregnant!"

Immediately my mother went home, pulled out the old family bible and opened it to Genesis 1:1. She took a newspaper, rolled it megaphone-style, and put the wide end to her stomach and spoke into the other end. She began reading from Genesis 1:1 all the way through the Apocrypha and then again half way through the Book of Numbers by the time I was born.

It was this remarkable woman who introduced me and brother to the riches of the "Good Book." Seated on the floor listening to my mother was our home entertainment system. The fact that your local library still sponsors story hours demonstrates that reading to a child has never really gone out of fashion as an intellectual activity. It also attests to the power of words and their ability to implant ideas and concepts deep into our psyche. The constant exposure to the Bible with its profound truths and timeless mysteries had a life-long impact. Sometimes, I couldn't wait for that little gathering after supper. I pulled out the Bible to see how the next installment was going to end. That's what happened one afternoon when I stumbled onto an intriguing passage in the Book of Maccabees.

In those days, it was not uncommon to pick up a King James Bible that included the Apocryphal books of the Maccabees. It was when I read the words from Second Book of Maccabees that I learned of the Ark being concealed by the prophet Jeremiah. I was about nine years old and the passage would haunt me for the rest of my life:

> "It is also found in the records, that Jeremiah, the prophet, commanded them that were carried away, to take of the fire as it was signified, and how the prophet, having given them The Law, charged them not to forget the commandments....It was also contained in the same records, that the Prophet, being warned of God, commanded the Tabernacle, and the Ark to go with him, as he went forth into the mountain where Moses climbed up, and saw the heritage of God. And when Jeremiah came thither, he found a hollow cave, wherein he laid the Tabernacle, and the Ark, and the Altar of incense, and so

stopped the door......As for that place, it shall be unknown until the time that God gather his people again together, and receive them unto mercy. Then shall the Lord show them these things, and the glory of the Lord shall appear...."
– II Maccabees 2:1-8

When my mother arrived home late that afternoon, I asked her, "Have any of these things been found?"

"No, not yet and if they had been, the world would certainly know about it," she replied.

With the kind of certainty that nine-year olds can muster, I told her, "If they are on this earth then I will find them!"

She held my gaze and moved to put an arm around me and said, "Yes, son, I know."

For those not familiar with the historical context of this tale, it was a time of terrible upheaval for the people of Judea. Jerusalem had fallen to the armies of King Nebuchadnezzar. The prophet Jeremiah was addressing the survivors of that siege. Many of them the best and brightest of Israel would soon be relocated far to the north, to the land of Babylon. Jeremiah was admonishing the captives to hold onto the commandments of God and not to fall prey to the lavish lifestyle they would encounter in this new metropolis.

Jeremiah spoke from experience. Years before, he had visited the capital on a discreet diplomatic mission and beheld the shining blue-tiled gate of Ishtar. He was a guest in the king's opulent palace and lush hanging gardens.

Jeremiah managed to remove Israel's holiest treasures to a cave, so that the hiding place of those sacred vessels would remain top secret — until the people were brought back to the land.

Even as a youngster I was fully acquainted with the complete list of these vessels made for the Tabernacle, fashioned literally in the shadow of Mount Sinai —and not simply the vessels, but the deep rituals attached to each of them. My mother, leaving nothing out, had read aloud the detailed descriptions of services performed by Aaron, the High Priest and brother of Moses. Seated there with my brother, I found something appealing about the Creator giving such awesome responsibilities to two siblings. With nothing to distract us, our young minds absorbed the exhaustive citation of every procedure necessary for the service of the Tabernacle.

However, there was one ritual that struck me as particularly curious and it stayed with me. It is found in the 19th chapter of Numbers. The Israelites were to find a perfectly red cow that had never felt a yoke on its neck. It was killed and entirely burnt.

If one reads the text completely, several key points emerge:

❑ The calf is perfect in every aspect and dedicated for this one purpose.

❑ The offering was different from any of the other sacrifices because nothing was removed nor was any of it eaten. The whole animal was burnt.

❑ The ashes would be gathered and used to make the water of purification.

❑ The water of purification was necessary for cleansing people and any item that had become ritually impure.

❑ The process made the pure impure, and the impure pure.

❑ It was to be a perpetual statute.

❑ A portion of the ashes were to be kept for Israel.

❑ The ashes were to be placed in some kind of vessel.

The final point, regarding a vessel is found in verse 17, but actually not stated clearly in the KJV rendering of Numbers 19. The text explains that the priest must take the ashes of the red cow and mix them with running water *in a vessel*. My young ears had mistakenly heard that the ashes alone were to be placed in a certain vessel. This idea was reinforced by verse 9, which indicates that a portion of the ashes would be retained as a memorial. The Jewish Sages tell us that a portion of the ashes were stored in the sanctuary of the Temple in Jerusalem.[1]

It was serendipity that I had misconstrued the meaning of those words concerning the ashes. I would learn later that this simple misunderstanding was actually the truth; the ashes were placed in a special container known as the *kalal*.

An Eternal Keepsake

"For I will take you from among the nations, and gather you from all countries, and will bring you into your own land. Then I will sprinkle clean water upon you, and you shall be clean from all your filthiness; and from all your idols, will I cleanse you. A new heart also will I give you, and a new spirit will I put inside you; and I will take away the heart of stone from your flesh, and I will give you a heart of flesh. And I will put my spirit inside you, and cause you to follow my statutes, and you shall keep my judgments, and do them. And you shall dwell in the land that I gave to your fathers; and you shall be my people, and I will be your God."
— Ezekiel 36:24-28

When the Ark of the Covenant, the *Mishkhan* (Tabernacle), and other sacred vessel are eventually recovered, they can only be handled by *kohanim* (priesthood) who have been purified. The Talmud reminds us that this was also strictly observed during the time of Solomon. Anyone entering *Beit Ha Mikdash* (First Temple) had to be ritually clean. You will note in the above passage from Ezekiel, there will come a day when the Chosen People will also need to be cleansed by "clean water," an almost redundant phrase. The process, as described in the previous chapter, is one of the least understood commandments in the Torah.

Technically, it is a *chokh*. Most of the commandments are actually *mitzvoth*, which are commonsense directives, such as not to eat certain animals or to commit murder. They make perfect sense. On the other hand, a *chokh* is a statute that appears to defy logic, but is followed without explanation. Though these ashes were necessary to cleanse anyone entering the Temple, even the wise Solomon confessed that this was a riddle that he could not comprehend:

> *"Amarti achakhema vehi rechokah mimeni,* ('I said I would acquire wisdom, but it is far from me')"
> — Ecclesiastes 7:23

Solomon was alluding to his inability to comprehend the profound paradoxes involved in the decree of the Red Cow. This connection is revealed in his use of the phrase *vehi rechokah*. Those words have the *gematria* (numerical value) of 441 which is the same gematria of the phrase *parah adumah* (red cow).

From the Talmudic commentaries, we can glean that only Moses fathomed the physical and spiritual properties of the process.[1] Some modern commentaries have theorized that mixing the ashes from a dead animal with living water is akin to a vaccine prepared from a strain of the disease it is meant to fight. On a mystical level, the Red Cow is linked to the sin of the Golden Calf. That idol was burnt then pulverized to a powder and mixed with water which the Israelites were forced to drink. The Red Cow was also completely burnt, processed into a powder, and added to water.

Red is the color of sin as alluded to in Isaiah 1:18:

"Though your sins be like scarlet, they shall be white as snow."

The ashes were prepared in the following manner. Moses was instructed to have a perfect red cow led outside the camp by Eleazar. There, it was to be slaughtered. The animal was then burnt with a mixture of cedar, hyssop, and scarlet coloring. This compound was finely sifted and a minute amount was mixed into water. It could be a vessel or even a large body of water. Purification occurred only if the surface of the water was disturbed upon contact with the ashes.

In the *Mishnah,* Tractate *Parah,* we learn that there have been a total of nine perfectly red cows burnt throughout history. The first was under the supervision of Moses; the second was prepared by Ezra; two by Shimon Ha Tzaddik; Yochanan, the High Priest also sacrificed two; Eliehoenai, the son of Ha-Kof was the seventh. Hanamel, the Egyptian, burnt the eighth. The ninth Red Cow was sacrificed by Ishmael, son of Piabi.

The tenth Red Heifer will be burnt in the time of *Messiach.*

During the First and Second Temples, the ashes were divided into thirds. One portion was given to the Levites guarding the entrance to the Temple. Another part was stored in the Mount of Olives; that share was used to purify the priests. That was required, if the priest needed to burn another red heifer. The remaining third was placed in a wall

The text on this 15th century plaque is attributed to R. Simon Bar Yochai, the 2nd century rabbi who wrote the Zohar. On the plaque it is written: "One gentile will purify himself, and they will sanctify the Name of mine. They will stand together side by side, hand in hand , shoulder to shoulder, heart in heart, under much duress and opposition, and will not stop until they have swept every corner and found her."

known as the *chail* which faced the Women's Gallery of the Temple. A portion of these ashes were to be undisturbed as it states in Numbers 19: 9-10, *"as a keepsake for Israel."*

In the *Siddur*, the Jewish prayer book, we find this fascinating prayer in the section of the Four Parshiot read at the beginning of Passover season:

"....Moses' cow would be eternal, for all the other cows would be used up, but yours will last forever." [2]

There has been disagreement, among some contemporary rabbinical figures, that those ashes stored away so long ago are of little importance. However, leading figures such the late Lubavitcher Rebbe Menachem Schneerson, Rabbi Adin Israel Steinsaltz, and Reuven Grodner (formerly of Hebrew University) all agree with the above stated condition from Mishna 5 — the ashes from the very first red cow were necessary to make the water of purification. Menachem Burstin, an Israeli botanist and expert on Biblical chemistry, has stated that he has isolated all of the necessary ingredients for preparing the water of purification — except for the ashes of the Red Cow.

The impact of this rite on the Jewish people of today is so significant that the Lubavitcher Rebbe, of Blessed Memory, stated:

"The Commandment of the Red Heifer represents the totality of the Torah."

Through the years, I would learn many of the specifics that I have detailed for you in the previous paragraphs. In my journey to uncover the ashes, I would also discover an essential link to the treasures of the *Mishkhan* (Tabernacle).

The Ashes of the Red Cow were placed in the *kalal*, a special container of burnished copper. Rabbi Maimonides Ben Moses, the esteemed Jewish sage known as the Rambam, states in his commentary *Parah* that the ashes were stored in the *kalal*.[3] The reference to this particular vessel did not escape the notice of Dead Sea Scroll's editor, John Allegro. In his book, *Treasure of the Copper Scroll*, he noted that:

> *"Interesting enough, the [Hebrew] word used by [the Copper Scroll] scribe as 'pitcher' coincides with that found in rabbinic tradition for the vessel containing the ashes of the sacrifice.... In rabbinic tractate dealing with regulations for the Red Heifer ceremony, there is a section concerned with the question of whether contact between a Biblical scroll and the pitcher used for sacrificial ashes affected the ritual cleanliness of the latter."*[4]

The word *kalal* appears in Column 6 on line 4 of the Copper Scroll.

Some researchers have mistakenly rendered this word as *kalil* which means a "curse." This is a patently silly notion, and has nothing to do with the context of the scroll. One is led to ask, how do you hide a curse, or why would anyone leave instructions where to locate a curse?

Ultimately, I hope to uncover all of the sacred treasures of the Copper Scroll. But the *kalal* containing the ashes will be pivotal if a new priesthood is to handle the holy objects fashioned at the foot of Mount Sinai just over three thousand years ago. I am convinced that they will be found in tandem with the purification — the Ashes of the Red Cow. The prayer from the *Siddur* has been a source of encouragement to those who have joined me through the years on this holy quest.

> *"The hiding place of the ashes will be revealed; from its deep mystery we will draw knowledge at the time when G-d will raise up the nation He protects.*[5]

That day I asked my mother about the hiding of the sacred treasures, pieces of a puzzle began to fall into place. My head swirled with a myriad of details and possibilities. It promised they would be found again.

Indeed, these items and the priests handling them would be purified.

The vessel containing the ashes had to be part of this sacred cache. It was enough to stir any youngster's imagination. But two simple words from the 2nd Chapter of II Maccabees tugged at some deeper place in me — *"other records."*

What records? Where are those records? I can not begin the search until I find those records!

The account of hiding the Ark and the Tabernacle is not found in the Bible. Knowledge of *other records,* outside of the Biblical canon that told this tale. I tucked that phrase away. It was one of those pivotal experiences that would dictate the direction of my whole life.

Notes

1 *Bamidbar Rabbah* 19:6

2 *Artscroll Siddur*, Mesorah Publications, Brooklyn, NY, 1985,p. 941

3 *Mishna, Parah* 3:3

4 Allegro, *The Treasure of the Copper Scroll*, Doubleday & Co, Garden City, New York, p.104, also see his reference to the *Qalal (Kalal)* in his endnote #126 p. 149

5 Artscroll Siddur, p.937

The Library
in the Wilderness

Thus says the Lord of hosts, the God of Israel;
Take these deeds, this deed of the purchase,
both the one which is sealed, and this deed which
is open; and put them in an earthen vessel,
that they may last for many days.
— Jeremiah 32:14

In the early winter of 1947, three Ta'amireh Bedouin were grazing their flocks north of a ruin called Qumran, along the shores of Israel's Dead Sea, when one of them stumbled on to a cache of writings secreted away over 2,000 years ago.

In this oft-told tale, Mohammed adh-Dhib was a dutiful youngster looking for a stray from his flock, but found instead, large clay vessels containing ancient scrolls. An alternate version relates that he was a young man in his 20's, and simply killing time by tossing rocks into a small crevice. Things got interesting when he heard the cracking of pottery. Later, in a recorded interview with John Trever (the first to ever photograph the scrolls), adh-Dhib would describe what he saw after falling into the cramped chamber which held the first and most complete of the Dead Sea Scrolls.

As the golden rays of the rising sun began to illuminate the cave, Mohammed saw ten large clay jars. He removed the lid from one of them and found three scrolls. The shepherd climbed from the cave and showed one of the scrolls to his cousin Jum'a[1] who was with the flock. They returned to the cave to inspect their new find. In all, there were seven scrolls in fairly well-preserved condition. It is at this point that most accounts either gloss over or ignore an intriguing detail.

Driven by their curiosity and possibly encountering a stubborn lid, the two young men proceeded to break open one of the jars, spilling out what they later describe as "red dirt."[2]

This begs the question, why would anyone take the trouble to stash dirt in a clay jar alongside sacred books?

I will address that question in another chapter.

Mohammed adh-Dhib, along with Jum'a Muhammed and Khalil Musa waited until the spring to offer their mysterious finds to a Bethlehem carpenter, Ibraham Ijha. But the amateur antiquities dealer was not interested. Another month passed until the scrolls were brought to the attention of a Khalil Eskander, better known as Kando the Cobbler. After a series of missteps, the scrolls finally found an interested party — a Syrian Orthodox monk known as Mar Athanasius Samuel.

A deal was cut with the monk. Kando sold him four of the scrolls for the bargain price of what would have been about $97.20. That sum was then shared with the Bedouin as agreed. These days, the son of Kando claims that his father kept one of the original jars and proudly displays the vessel in the family's east Jerusalem antique shop.[3]

Cave #4 adjacent to Wadi Qumran. Because numerous books and television documentaries feature this site, most people have the mistaken impression that this is the cave where the Bedouin shepherd made his wonderful discovery in 1947.

Another merchant from Bethlehem, Faidi Salahi, would later acquire another two scrolls. The Syrian monk subsequently offered his valuable purchase to a series of experts who all deemed them as having little value.

By late November, Professor Eliezar Sukenik, founder of the Institute of Archaeology at Hebrew University in Jerusalem, learned of the scrolls. Inspecting them would require that Sukenik travel to Bethlehem which was risky business for any Jew. Hostilities were expected any day because of the upcoming United Nations decision to partition Palestine. The militants among the Arab population were unhappy about the prospect.

Details are somewhat murky but most accounts tell of
the brave Sukenik, disguised in a kafiyah, taking the bus to
Bethlehem so that he could verify that the scrolls were
genuine.

On November 29th, Sukenik borrowed the scrolls to take
home and examine. They were the *Book of Isaiah, Thanksgiving Hymns* and *The War of the Sons of Light Against the
Sons of Darkness*. That night as he examined his prizes, the
professor heard the radio broadcast announcing the majority
vote in the United Nations, allowing the partition of Palestine.
This momentous vote would lead to the creation of the
modern State of Israel. The coincidence and its impact were
not lost on Sukenik.

The news of this extraordinary discovery began to slowly
ripple into other scholarly circles in the region. The
international press picked up the story in April of 1948. Weeks
later, the story was quickly overshadowed by an even bigger
event.

On May 14, 1948, the British High Commissioner sailed
out of the port of Haifa, signaling the last gasp of Her
Majesty's grip on the Promised Land. It was the end of
the British Mandate in Palestine. At 4:00 pm that same
day, David Ben-Gurion read the nation's Declaration of
Independence. Just two hours later, the United States officially
recognized Israel as a sovereign nation.[4]

With the birth of modern Israel came its first struggle for survival. Israel's enemies dropped bombs at dawn the next day. The War of Independence had officially begun. Defending the fledgling nation as General Chief of Staff for the Israeli army was Yigal Yadin, the son of Eliezer Sukenik. Like his father, Yadin would later join the ranks of the country's leading archaeologists.

Israel survived the onslaught of five Arab nations and got down to the business of building a democracy in the Middle East. Following the war, there was renewed interest in the discoveries at Qumran. But by January of 1949, none of the original characters involved with the initial discovery of scrolls would reveal the location of the cave. A Belgian UN Observer, Captain Phillipe Lippens, was keenly interested in the whereabouts of the original cave and managed to stoke the interest of the British authorities. They were convinced to contact the head of the Jordanian Antiquities Authority. Soon, a small team was dispatched to have a look. Most accounts credit Captain Akkash al-Zebn for relocating the site now known as Cave Q1.[5]

The first season of archaeological excavations began near Khirbet Qumran led by Gerald Lankester Harding, an Englishman who had been the head of the Jordanian Antiquities Department since 1936. Also on hand was Father Roland de Vaux from École Biblique, an archaeological school housed in the old Dominican Monastery of St. Stephen in Jerusalem. De Vaux would eventually head up the International Scroll Team.

Photo courtesy of: The Gerald Lankester Harding Archive
Gerald Lankester Harding (4th from left), Director of the Antiquities of the Hashemite Kingdom of Jordan and Pere Roland de Vaux from Archeologique de Jerusalem with a detail of Jordanian soldiers sent to guard the excavations at Qumran.

As exploration continued, other caves would surrender more ancient documents. This sprawling depository of knowledge would eventually yield over 850 scrolls.

Worldly Delights

It was accepted almost from the very beginning that the various writings represented a kind of forgotten library. If that is the case, then these scrolls should represent what one finds on any library shelf: copies as well as originals of books and documents. Like any library, some collected works would offer the same subject matter. Like any library, there will be books that come from different time periods.

This last notion seems to have been quickly discarded by the Scroll Team. They arbitrarily deemed the scrolls the product of roughly the same time period and all the product of a team of scribes. It was also accepted, without question that those who produced the scrolls inhabited the settlement of Qumran when Rome ruled over Judea.

Surprisingly, it was Professor Sukenik who first offered the theory that the scrolls were authored by a sect called the Essenes. Though there is not even a hint of the word Essene on any scrap of parchment found among the caves in that dusty arid region of Judea, the École Biblique seized on what is still very much a theory. They and their supporters consider it axiomatic that the authors of the Dead Sea Scrolls were Essenes and that they were also the first Christians. However, even as I write these words, more than fifty years after the fact, the debate still rages as to who actually resided at Qumran. One theory suggests that it is the remains of a Roman villa while another view holds that it was a military outpost.

It is altogether possible that the site might have been, during various times in history, the habitation of any number of groups of varying demographics. I'm sure the Bedouin even spent some time there, sheltering their livestock.

In a monumental display of what Freudian psychology calls "projection," the ascetics at École Biblique could only see the handiwork of proto-monks who, like them, were supposed to shun women and other worldly delights. École Biblique controlled the scrolls and so it seems that this was the frame of reference that would color Dead Sea Scrolls research from the very beginning. Years later, writing for *Vanity Fair*, Ron Rosenbaum would characterize the situation in this way:

> *"They had the power to limit access to the texts to themselves and whichever favored few graduate students and acolytes they blessed with a precious fragment. Privileged access became the basis of lifelong academic careers, scholarly empire building; the Scrolls were the hot center of contemporary biblical studies and Scroll scholars became powerful, globe-trotting academic superstars."[6]*

The Isaiah Scroll on display in Jerusalem at the Shrine of the Book

This state of affairs persisted for nearly fifty years until the release of several pivotal texts finally revealed the rich Jewish character of the Dead Sea Scrolls. Today, the scrolls are divided into three general categories. There are scriptural texts and a portion of writings called "apocryphal." Another section of works embrace aspects of conduct in the community.[7]

One thing all of these writings have in common is their very Kosher character. A contemporary observant Jew can read the scrolls and be struck by the continuity for many of his beliefs stretching back to antiquity. It permeates the Scrolls. He could also examine the little leather *tefillin*, (phylacteries) found in those same caves and note that they were constructed in the same fashion as those he dons for his daily prayers.

Flavius Josephus , a Jewish historian who was born the same year that the Roman despot Caligula took the throne, is one of three writers of that era who inform us of a Jewish sect called Essenes.[8]

As described by Josephus, these men didn't think much of marriage and viewed wives as a hindrance. At first blush, this view of women appears to be shared by the authors of the Scrolls. It is the most misunderstood aspect of these documents because of the number of strictures placed on male members of the community found in the sectarian writings that deal with everyday life. But that is also what you will find in the Torah.

Ask any observant Jew and they will tell you that the majority of *mitzvoth* (laws) in the Torah are very much directed at the male of the species. Less is expected of a Jewish woman because in the view of the Creator, as found in the Torah, she is built for nurturing and caring, and possesses an innate wisdom. On the other hand, men have to work at being spiritual. For that reason, most of the guidelines in the Community Rules are directed at the men folk.

Nowhere in the Dead Sea Scrolls is there a commandment for celibacy. On the contrary, there are texts that support Torah law forbidding a *kohen* (priest) from marrying the wrong kind of partner. The document known as 4QMMT underscores the need for the *kohanim* (priesthood), the Sons of Aaron, to marry with certain provisions:

> *"They are holy, and the sons of Aaron are [most holy]. But you know that some of the priests and [the laity mingle with each other]...[And they]unite with each other and pollute the [holy] seed [as well as]as their own [seed] with women whom they are forbidden to marry.*   — *4QMMTT (B79-92)*

Now compare the above lines with the mitzvah given to the *kohanim* in the book of Leviticus:

> *"They shall not take a wife who is a harlot, or defiled; nor shall they take a woman put away from her husband; for he is holy to his God...And he shall take a wife in her virginity. A widow, or a divorced woman, or defiled, or a harlot, these shall he not take; but he shall take a virgin of his own people to wife. Neither shall he defile his seed among his people; for I the Lord do sanctify him."*   — Leviticus 21:7-15

These laws were necessary because the *kohanim* were held to a much higher standard than the rest of the community of Israel. As you can see from the line in the above verse, *"...he shall take a virgin of his own people...,"* the men of the tribe of Levi were not allowed to marry outside of the tribe. This was for the sake of preserving the priestly line and keeping it whole. There is ample evidence that this was practiced at one time. Genetic research has found that Jews who can claim ancestry to the priestly tribe of Levi all have their own distinctive gene marker that is not found among other Jews.[9]

Much as been made of the water system and ritual baths at Qumran, however, an observant Jew, whether in antiquity or present day is commanded to make regular visits to a *mikvah* for cleansing oneself for a variety of reasons.[10] Jewish women must go to the *mikvah* at least once a month.

The famous Damascus Document found in the Cairo Geniza[11] aids us in further clarification. The other appellation given to this precious document is the Zadokite Fragments, so-called because of the references to the Levitical lineage known as the Sons of Zadok. The tomb of Zadok, a genuine historical personage from the First Temple era, is referenced directly in the Copper Scroll.

The Zadokite texts are often referred to as the "First Dead Sea Scrolls" because they were discovered in 1897 in Old Cairo in the Ben Ezra Synagogue by Dr. William Bowen of Cambridge. This site is famous for having been the synagogue of the great Jewish sage Maimonides (the Rambam). Legend has it that it was built on the very spot where the infant

Moses was drawn from the Nile in his little reed ark. This vast accumulation of Jewish literature was taken to Cambridge by Solomon Schechter where the collection remains today.

The impact of the Damascus Document is undeniable. The references to the Sons of Zadok make for a solid connection to the Dead Sea Scrolls. For instance, one of the very first scrolls found at Qumran in Cave 1 also mentions the Sons of Zadok. It's important to remember that Zadok was the *Kohen Gadol* (High Priest) in the time of Solomon. He and his descendants were the designated order who would continue the priestly line. According to Ezekiel 44:9, the Zadokite line was set apart and authorized to direct the worship in the future temple. That anticipated house of worship is detailed in the Temple Scroll found in Cave 11 and eventually recovered by Yigal Yadin.

I don't want to nag but since the Zadokite Fragments are indeed tied to the documents found at Qumran then we can quickly dispel any notions that the authors were against marriage. As Lawrence Schiffman points out in his aptly titled *Reclaiming the Dead Sea Scrolls*:

> *"On the contrary, the Zadokite Fragments contain many indications of a society in which marriage and family were the norm."*[12]

Here's just one of those indications that Schiffman quotes from the Zadokite texts:

"If they live in camps according to the custom of the land, and they have taken wives and had children, then they should live according to Torah"   — Zadokite Fragments 7:6-7[13]

Evidence of women and children in an allegedly celibate community at Qumran; a priestly lineage in service to the First Temple, and the discovery of the Temple Scroll are all vital elements that fueled my own decades-long quest for holy treasures painstakingly etched onto the Copper Scroll and hidden near the Dead Sea, in the Valley of Achor.

Notes

1 Some published accounts reveal that J'uma was the first to spy the cave but did not go inside, see *Understanding the Dead Sea Scrolls*, Harry Thomas Frank, Ed. Hershel Shanks, Random House, NY, 1992, p.5

2 John Trever, *Untold Story of Qumran*, Fleming H. Revell Company, Westwood NJ, 1946, p.170

3 Dennis Eisenberg, *The Jinni's Curse*, Jerusalem Post International, August 2, 1997, p.14

4 Editors of the New York Times, *Israel: The Historical Atlas*, Macmillan Publishing, USA, p.48

5 Trever, Untold Story of Qumran, Fleming H. Revell Company, Westwood, NJ 1946, p.121

6 Rosenbaum, *The Riddle of the Scrolls*, Vanity Fair, November 1992, p.287

7 Lawrence H. Schiffman, *Reclaiming the Dead Sea Scrolls*, Doubleday, NY, 1994, p.33

8 Josephus is a fascinating figure. He was a Pharisee who could trace his lineage to the Hashmonean kings. After surviving the wars against Rome, he was commissioned to record the history of the Jewish people. His works are highly regarded today and have been authenticated by archaeological finds in Israel.

9 Judy Siegel, *Genetic Link Found Among Kohanim*, Jerusalem Post International, January 11, 1997, p.32

10 Much of Leviticus, chapter 15 deals with the laws of the mikvah.

11 A *geniza* is a depository for sacred Jewish texts which, when damaged or aged, must be either stored or buried.

12 Schiffman, *Reclaiming the Dead Sea Scrolls*, Doubleday, NY, 1994, p.130

13 Ibid, p.131

A Scroll
Unlike Any Other

*I left Professor Baker that night longing to try out
his machine on the first scroll, now unpacked and
lying on the table alongside. It was agreed that he
should make the first cut the following morning,
but I was not unduly surprised to hear his voice on
the telephone late that evening, telling me,
between gasps of air, that he had done it. The roll
had not shattered into a thousand pieces; the first
segment
now lay open to the light.*
— The Treasure of the Copper Scroll
by John Marco Allegro

The Bedouin got paid less than a hundred dollars for
finding the first set of Dead Sea Scrolls. Hoping to land a
bigger payday, they joined renewed efforts to uncover
more archaeological riches spurred on by the discovery
of a second cave at Qumran. The excavation was led by Gerald
Lankester Harding, Director of the Jordanian Antiquities
Authority in cooperation with École Biblique, the Palestine
Archaeological Museum and the American Schools of
Oriental Research, or ASOR.

According to the published reports, on March 14th, 1952,
a third cave was located by Henri de Contenson. The
chamber was only 9 or 10 yards deep and just north of Cave
1Q.[1] Inside the collapsed chamber were dozens of empty clay

jars, bones and some scraps of parchment. On March 20th, the Copper Scroll was found in the two segments, stacked one on top of the other. It was obvious that these segments had been there since antiquity because they were lodged against the wall of the cave by a massive boulder.

This was the only scroll found in Israel, even to this day, made from copper. The metal had almost completely oxidized and was therefore extremely brittle. Any attempt to unroll the artifact would cause the folds to shatter. The team decided to wait before attempting to open this curiosity. For a while, this new find would languish under glass in a Jerusalem museum.

Enter a Professor K.G. Kuhn, visiting from Heidelberg. According to John Allegro's colorful description, Kuhn spent hours gazing at this metallic curiosity, taking notes and decoding the Hebrew characters that seemed to tease with words such "gold," "silver" and "buried."[2] At this point, no one seemed interested in what Kuhn had to say about the scroll. It remained an enigma for many years.

When John Allegro joined the Scroll Team in Jerusalem, the mysteries of the Copper Scroll beckoned to him. He convinced Harding, that the necessary resources for opening the scroll might be found back in England at the Manchester College of Science and Technology, where Allegro often lectured.

Finally, in the spring of 1955, Harding was able to secure permission to release one of two coiled sections to Allegro. By that summer, Allegro had joined forces with Professor H. Wright Baker, the professor of Mechanical Engineering. They fashioned a machine that would saw the scroll, now known as 3Q15[3], into segments. Before slicing into the artifact, they coated it with an aircraft adhesive to prevent any of the segments from fragmenting.

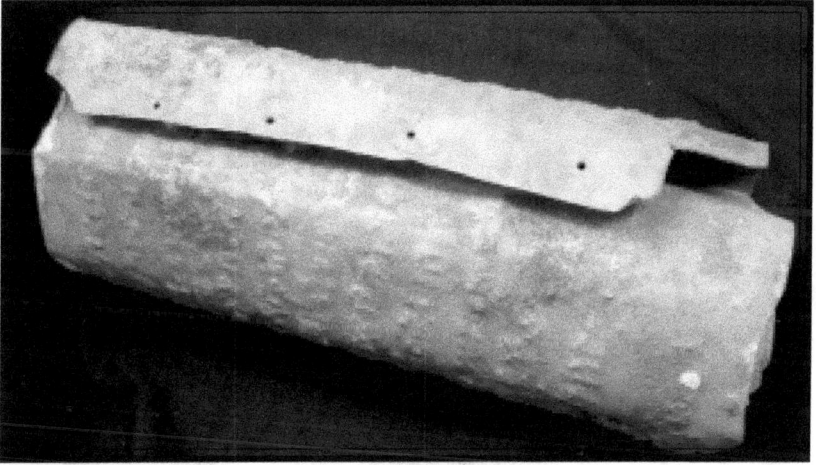

After testing the shaky, Rube Goldberg device, Allegro and Baker called it a night. But, as Allegro later revealed in his book on the Copper Scroll, apparently Baker's curiosity got the best of him and he sawed into the scroll that night. The machine had worked just fine. Later, when the work of Baker's home-grown scroll saw was finished, the Copper Scroll lay in 23 slightly curled segments. Now the contents could be read for the first time in over two-thousand years.[4]

Before we move on to the next chapter, I want to add an additional note on the discovery of the Copper Scroll. Not to steal Monsieur de Contenson's thunder, but there is someone else who maintains they found the Copper Scroll. The details were made known to me by an elderly Bedouin, claiming to be the very same

Mohammed ahd-Dhib as he appeared in 1997. At the time he was one of three men who claimed to be the shepherd who discovered the Dead Sea Scrolls in Cave 1.

Mohammed adh-Dhib who stumbled on Cave 1Q. He further claims that, in addition to finding Cave 1 and its historic cache, he also found the Copper Scroll. We do know that the scholars had employed about two dozen Bedouin from ahd-Dhib's tribe, the Ta'amireh, to help dig through some 275 caves during March of that year.[5]

Jim Long, of Lightcatcher Productions, videotaped an interview that I conducted with the old man near Qumran in January of 1997. Serving as interpreter was Musa, my trusted Bedouin friend who runs the camel concession at the Qumran tourist site.[6]

This Mohammed, at the time of the interview, was in his seventies. He stated that he had found the Copper Scroll and that the discovery was made in a different cave, much closer to Cave 1

.

During the course of the interview, despite the heat and his advanced years, the old man exhibited an amazing dexterity on the slopes of a very rocky ascent with relative ease. He stated that he made his home in Bethlehem then pointed to a small cave with a hole in the roof. We had to crawl on our knees into the mouth of the little cave. Once inside, he showed us where the team had found 45 jars, all empty save for 4 of them. He motioned us over to a slight depression on the floor of the cave. It was there, according to Mohammed, that he found the Copper Scroll, buried beneath a large stone. He also claimed that Harding paid him 10 Jordanian *dinar* for the find.

The little chamber shown to us during the interview is less than ten meters from Cave 11 where the Temple Scroll was found. It is also below the Spice Cave excavated by our own teams in 1992. If the little chamber pointed out during the interview was the real Copper Scroll cave, the implications are dramatic but not surprising because, as you will see, the Copper Scroll is linked with the finds of these two caves.

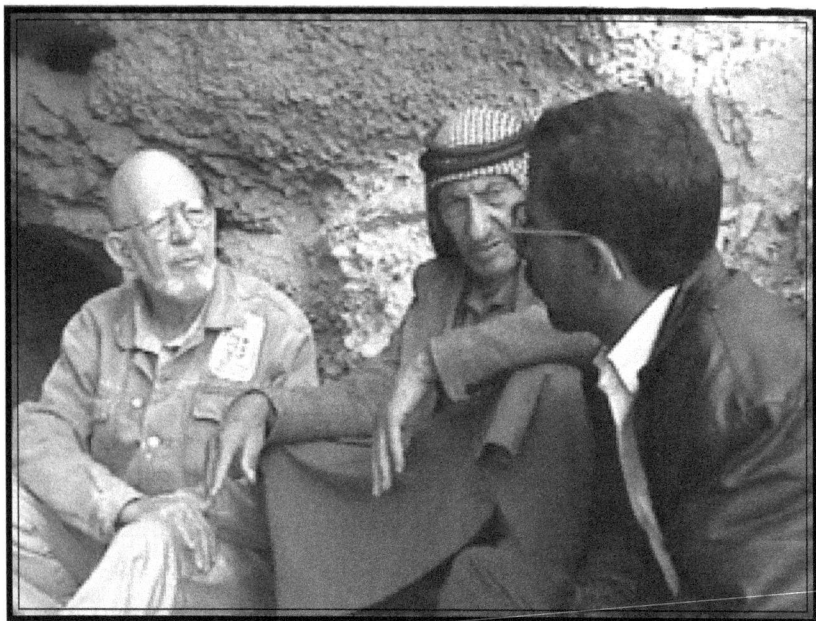

My old friend, Musa (on the right), acts as our interpreter as we interview Mohammed at Qumran.

The reader should be aware that one other man, and possibly a third, also claim to be *THE* shepherd Mohammed adh-Dhib who found the original Cave 1 and the Scrolls inside. One of them passed away in Amman, Jordan, in 1994.[7] He went to his deathbed claiming that he had been cursed by the *jinni* that guarded the caves:

"There were eight jars there...We were disappointed because we thought we would find a treasure of gold...we could see that the bundles were covered with linen smeared with a kind of black sticky stuff which had a bad smell...I should have listened to the warning in my heart. I knew that the jinni I had disturbed from his sleep was angry. I wanted to throw all the bundles into a fire, but the other boys stopped me."[8]

Note, in the above quote, that this Mohammed ahd-Dhib mentions finding only eight jars while most accounts report that there were at least ten jars in that first cave. Possibly we should attribute the discrepancy to advancing years and failing health.

Keep in mind that none of this can be proven. If this tale were true, it implies that the Scroll team had arbitrarily named another location, to confuse treasure hunters. As you will see in the next chapter, the International Scroll Team was so alarmed by the vast amounts of wealth promised by the Copper Scroll that they continued, for years, to diminish the veracity of the text. That might also give them ample reason to change the actual location of the find — a decoy to throw off potential looting?

Notes

[1] John Marco Allegro, The Treasure of the Copper Scroll, Anchor Books, New York, 1964, p.2

[2] Allegro, The Treasure of the Copper Scroll, Doubleday & Company, New York, 1960, p.22

[3] Tagged like exhibits in a court case, the artifacts are labeled according to the cave number and the order in which they were found in that cave.

[4] Allegro, p.24

[5] John Trever, The Dead Sea Scrolls, A Personal Account, Wm. Eerdmans Publ, Grand Rapids, MI, p.151

[6] If you are one of those fortunate enough to have visited Qumran and had your picture taken sitting astride a camel, you have probably met Musa or his brother, Ibrahim.

[7] Dennis Eisenberg, The Jinni's Curse, Jerusalem Post International, August 2, 1997, p.14

[8] ibid

Chiseled in Stone

And the Lord answered me, and said, Write the
vision, and make it plain upon tablets,
so that he who reads it may run.
— Habakkuk 2:2

The Dead Sea Scrolls were inscribed by pious Jews living in Israel thousands of years ago. The Jews of modern Israel had to pay a quarter of a million dollars to get their own ancient scrolls back. Though this is the kind of thing that drives the antiquities market (some would say Black Market) at least the people of Israel don't have to quibble with anyone over the ownership of the Dead Sea Scrolls.

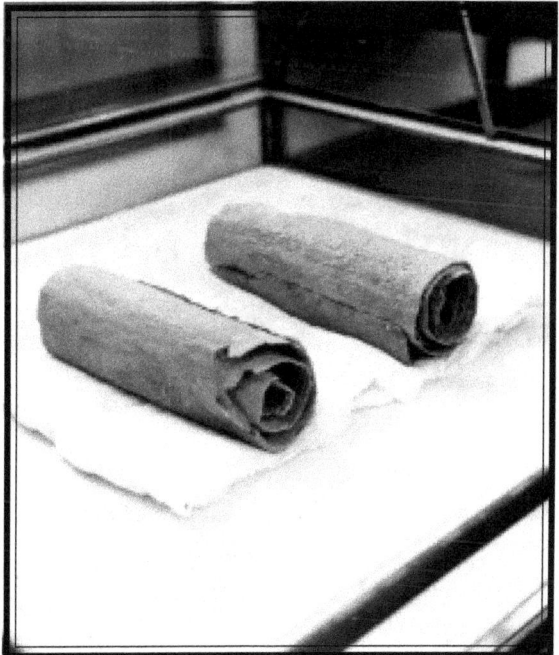

The Copper Scroll aka 3Q15 was found in two rolls when first discovered. Here are the sections just prior to being cut open in Manchester.

Photo credit:
Allegro Archives

Incredibly, the Copper Scroll remains the property of the Jordanian government. The site of its discovery, on the eastern shore of the Dead Sea, was under Jordanian control in 1952. But, for some reason, there has been no attempt to retrieve the scroll from Jordan. As far I know there has been no attempt to purchase the Copper Scroll or have it returned by diplomatic negotiations. Even more curious is why the people of Jordan would care about an artifact that is so obviously Jewish.

Controversy continues to swirl around the Copper Scroll. It remains the most unique, and for some, the most impenetrable of the Dead Sea Scrolls. Baffled by its contents, the Scroll team withheld news of its discovery for four years.

Some of the segments of the Copper Scroll on display in the Jordan Archaeological Museum in Amman.

In 1956, the world finally learned of the Copper Scroll, but it would be four more years before a complete English translation was available. The first translations resulted in the typical hand-wringing that often greets genuine archaeological discoveries that are not easily classifiable. The professional skeptics labeled this unique document "the work of a madman...a forgery...Jewish folklore...the writing of a charlatan who did not know Hebrew." The list goes on.

Scroll Team member, Father Josef Milik, published a partial rendering of the Copper Scroll in French. In a 1956 article, he went out of his way to dispel any notions that the contents of the scroll had any merit:

> "It goes almost without saying that the document is not an historical record of actual treasures buried in antiquity. The characteristics of the document itself, not to mention the fabulous quantity of precious metal recorded in it, place it firmly in the genre of folklore. The Copper Scroll is thus best understood as a summary of popular traditions circulating among the folk of Judea, put down by a semi-literate scribe."[1]

John Allegro had actually done his own translation of the scroll when it was in his possession at Manchester. He later offered the first full blown English rendering which hit the bookstores in 1960. His version of the Scroll detailed what is still considered, by some scholars, to be an overwhelming inventory of gold and silver — possibly too much to be taken seriously.

Father de Vaux and Milik were convinced that Allegro would stir up the kind of wild speculation they hoped to avoid. Though Milik's work on the Copper Scroll is a classic of scholarship, it is colored by theological views of his bosses at École Biblique. Allegro stood apart from his colleagues on the Scroll Team because he believed that text was genuine. He was convinced enough to launch his own search for the treasures of the Scroll. His exploration took him to Jerusalem and the Judean wilderness in the winter of 1959, and again in the spring of 1960. But he searched without success.

All of this squabbling — and there was much of it — that could be tied to the status of the Copper Scroll, would eventually be the cause of a great divide between De Vaux and Allegro. It almost seems that the more Allegro challenged the official view that the Copper Scroll was simply legendary, the more entrenched these scholars became.

Jewish sacred texts are often diminished by some scholars who assert that they are simply nothing more than myth. In their view, the entire *Tanakh* (Hebrew Bible) is a colorful collection of homilies and fables. They will also inform you, for instance, that the Flood of Noah is a tale borrowed from other cultures.

Milik, a priest, should have accorded the Copper Scroll at least a little respect. Instead, he consigned it to the realm of fantasy. To support this viewpoint, he compared it to an intriguing artifact discovered in the Beirut Museum some years earlier. In the museum's vaults were tablets, made of marble, inscribed with a text known as the *Masseket Kelim*, the Tractate of the Temple Vessels.[2]

This astonishing medieval Jewish *Midrash* relates how the Levites, led by five *Zadokim* (righteous men), buried the holy treasures of Solomon's Temple so that they would not fall into the hands of Babylonian hordes who would descend on Jerusalem.

The Rest of the Story

Midrash describes certain works or passages derived from the Oral Tradition now found in the Talmud and other Jewish sources. *Midrash* can be described as an "explanation." The word is derived from the Hebrew root *drash* which means the same as our English word "thrash." Add the Hebrew letter *mem*, meaning "from," and you get literally "from thrashing." This should give you some sense of how Midrash is the **kernel of truth** that is implied in the text. Midrash can also be the actual details of an event that were originally transmitted orally.

The Marble Tablets were found by Milik's compadre, Father Jean Starcky, who would also join the Scroll Team. Milik used the *Massaket Kelim* to build a case against the Copper Scroll. Since *Masseket Kelim* is an exhaustive and detailed list of sacred treasures, Father Milik maintained that it was without question a work of fiction. For him, the Copper Scroll fell into the same category since it also listed fabulous treasures. **The Copper Scroll was also directly mentioned in *Masseket Kelim*.** In one fell swoop, these men of the cloth decided that the Marble Tablets and the Copper Scroll represented nothing more than Jewish fairy tales. If that were true, then you have to give the Jewish sages credit for taking their fiction seriously enough to chisel pages of it onto stone and metal.

The Jordan Archaeological Museum where the
Copper Scroll remains on exhibit today.

Since I do accord a great amount of respect to the Jewish Sages of old, and I do believe they were serious people who spent their time on earth doing what they believed was God's work, I found it fascinating and vastly encouraging that the Marble Tablets make direct reference to the Copper Scroll. As I was to discover years later, there was another supporting text published by a Jewish sage who wanted the world to remember the treasures of the Copper Scroll.

Notes
1 Milik, *The Copper Document*, Biblical Archaeologist, September 1956, p. 63
2 Al Wolters, *Apocalyptic and the Copper Scoll*, Journal of Near Eastern Studies, Vol. 49, Jan/Oct 1990, University of Chicago Press, p.147

The Dream

*And it shall come to pass afterward, that I will
pour out my Spirit upon all flesh; and your sons
and your daughters shall prophesy, your old men
shall dream dreams, your young men shall see
visions: and also upon the servants and upon the
handmaids in those days will I pour out my Spirit.
And I will show wonders in the heavens and in the
earth, blood, and fire and pillars of smoke.*
— Joel 2:28-30

In 1945, I would catch a glimpse of my destiny as I sat
in the Sudan Theater in my home town. Those were the days
before television, when we got our news from broadcast radio
and newspapers. We looked forward to going to the movies
on the weekends so we could catch the latest Pathe or
Movietone newsreels. I will never forget what I saw in that
tiny cinema at the end of the war. It was the latest newsreel,
and it showed General Eisenhower touring what remained
of the Ohrdruf-Nord compound, one of the infamous Nazi
Death Camps.

Like others around me, I sat in stunned silence. The light
from the screen washed over me with hideous images of
brutalized Jewish bodies stacked like cords of wood, and
mass graves filled with even more corpses. There were the
haunted faces of the emaciated survivors. We were all
confronted with the terrible realization that humans did this
to other human beings. And it had been done because they
were Jews.

There in the dark, I recalled how my mother had always spoken with affection for the Jewish people and of their role as a nation chosen by God — to be a kingdom of priests who would eventually minister to the needs of our entire world. I still believed those words, even as the horror on the theater screen jolted me to tears. I resolved that I would somehow do my part to prevent another Holocaust.

Three years later, I was a tall, lanky field hand doing my best to make a living. That's when I first heard about the discovery of the Dead Sea Scrolls. It was in April that the story finally made its way into newspapers and magazines. They had been found in a region with the exotic sounding name of Qumran.

Could these be the *other records* mentioned in Second Maccabees?

It would take a few more years to find out what those first scrolls contained. In the meantime, I had to make my way in the world. That summer found me working with my uncle, Clyde Wainscott, as we literally cut a swath from Texas to Canada, gathering the wheat harvest. It was dry enough that we were able to operate the Case combines all day and into the night. That meant a non-stop schedule of eighteen-hour days running endlessly. The only thing that would halt our work was rainfall.

I was exhausted and prayed, "Please Lord, let it rain!"

Finally, it rained just outside of Paducah, Texas.

We drove into town and ate heartily. The effect of the large meal and fatigue rapidly took its toll on me.

"I'm gonna go get some sleep in the pick-up," I told my Uncle Clyde, "so please don't wake me up for anything or anybody!"

I don't know if I could have taken another step. Somehow, I managed to pull off my sweaty work shirt and shed my socks and shoes before tumbling headlong into some of the sweetest slumber I had ever experienced.

That was when the dream came.

I was standing with a multitude somewhere on a hill. We were bathed in a glowing light. A fanfare sounded from silver trumpets. The sound of the horns grew louder and louder. There were angels in front of us. Their eyes shone as they sang — their words were stirringly beautiful and rang with a triumphant, joyful sound — even though they were in a language I could not comprehend. I felt an undercurrent of anticipation as a shout went up. All eyes turned toward a hill where six men in flowing garments hoisted a brilliant golden box topped with images of winged creatures. There was loud banging but this sound was harsher, with a more metallic report. Though I fought to hold on to the dream, I awoke to someone banging on the front of the truck.

"Vendyl, get out here. You need to hear this!" a voice exclaimed.

It was my Uncle surrounded by the boys from the crew. He had the Lubbock newspaper spread across the hood, one corner anchored by a lunch pail, the other by an open Bible.

Nobody ever called my uncle by his given name, Clyde. To everyone that knew him, he was "The Preacher." My uncle was neither a man of the cloth nor any kind of ordained minister. He didn't even have a congregation, but his knowledge of the Bible was encyclopedic. If you asked him a question about the Bible, he could literally quote you chapter and verse.

I slunk from the cab of the truck, trying to orient myself. I sluggishly listened as my uncle read a news item then turned to a related passage in the Bible. He was in full Preacher form as he cited a story about the latest atomic bomb tests and he linked it to the prophecies in Joel that warned of "blood, fire and pillars of smoke."

He pointed to another item relating the latest UFO sighting, somewhere near the Panhandle (Roswell had already made headlines the previous summer), again referring to the prophet Joel's references to "signs and wonders in the heavens."

But the biggest story in that day's edition was the dispatch telling how on the 14th of May, 1948, the modern state of Israel had been established.

Uncle Clyde flipped the pages of his Bible and jabbed a finger towards the book saying, "It's all in there boys. The old prophets said that the Jewish people would return to their land."

I leaned over the hood and slid the worn leather volume toward me. It was open to the book of Amos. I began reading the 9th verse in the 9th chapter; God would *"sift the house of Israel among all the nations, like corn, yet not lose a single grain."* I could appreciate the agricultural character of the passage. It seemed to hit closer to home since my life those past few days was spent reclaiming grains of wheat from their stalks. I continued to read, struck by the immediacy of the words in the last two verses of the book of Amos:

"And I will bring again the captivity of my people of Israel, and they shall build the waste cities and inhabit them; and they shall plant vineyards, and drink wine thereof; they shall also make gardens, and eat the fruit of them.

"And I will plant them upon their land, and they shall no more be pulled up out of their land which I have given them, saith the Lord thy God."   — Amos 9:14-15

The chosen people of Israel, the Jews, had returned to their own land after 2,000 years, just as written by "the old prophets." I looked from the pages of the Bible back to the newspaper headlines. I could sense my role in this drama dimly taking form.

A few months later, in 1949, the November 21st issue of the New York Times would feature a small story briefly noting that when Israel became a state, the Jewish population in the land was just over 600,000.[1]

For anyone who knows their Bible, this was an amazing figure. According to the scripture, Israel's census of adult males when they departed Egypt during the Exodus was also over 600,000.[2]

Notes

1 *Israel: The Historical Atlas*, compiled by the Editors of the NY Times, MacMillan Publishing, USA, 1997, p. 55
2 Exodus 12:37

Never A Preacher

*"I'm uncomfortable with the thought of this
Jewish ritual. Are you sure it's necessary?"*
- Nazi Officer, just before opening the Ark,
from the film *Raiders of the Lost Ark*

I began my studies in theology by enrolling at Southwest Theological Seminary in 1950. My mother didn't seem all that impressed with my decision but remained philosophical, *"I guess it's as good as any place to start. But it's not where you're going to finish."*

I pursued my Masters in Divinity by transferring to Bible Baptist Seminary in Fort Worth. I was there until 1954 and from time to time, I would catch snippets of information about more discoveries at Qumran, which had yet to be disclosed to the world at large. There were even whispers of a scroll unlike any of the others. Not a book — but a Copper Scroll with a list of fabulous sacred wealth.

I needed to ground myself in the essentials of archaeology so I took my degree and headed for Bob Jones University. I have taken considerable heat for attending Bob Jones, a school with a well-earned reputation for blatantly Bible-thumping backwardness. But I wasn't interested in their theology. I wanted to learn from an unsung hero who quietly worked among their ranks. He was Dr. William Bowen, the curator of a small but unique museum that bore his name. Bowen and his wife had studied and worked with two pioneers in archaeology: Sir William Flinders Petrie and William Foxwell Albright.

Petrie helped establish the study known as Egyptology and came into his own at the end of the 19th Century. He surveyed the Great Pyramid at Giza and conducting the first digs at such important archaeological sites as Abydos and Tel al-Amarna in Egypt. He developed a solid methodology for studying and classifying artifacts. Petrie trained a new breed of scholars who blazed trails in the young discipline called "archaeology" and ranged from Egypt to Israel in his quest for knowledge.

W.F. Albright would make a name for himself in the field of Biblical Archaeology during the 1920's with his excavations in Israel. He was well versed in linguistics, the Bible and his study of ancient ceramics did much to advance the study of archaeology. Albright worked for years in the Middle East as Director of the American School of Oriental Research and is probably best known for authenticating the Dead Sea Scrolls found in Cave Q1.

Dr. Bowen's own experience was hard-won from years of toil and study, digging in the Middle East alongside these two giants of archaeology. He imparted to me his valuable and practical knowledge of identifying pottery, and schooled me in the fundamentals of excavating. He stressed the importance of knowing both the geology and geography of Biblical Israel. But Dr. Bowen was more than a teacher. He was my mentor.

By 1955, I had moved to the tree-covered hills of Northeast Tennessee and made my home in mountainous scenic Carter County, right on the State line of Virginia. I became pastor of the Dungan Chapel Baptist Church. I was never a preacher, never considered myself a man of the cloth or a Reverend. My real love was teaching. But even the beauty of nearby Roan Mountain did not quell my restlessness, especially when the existence of the Copper Scroll was confirmed. The news of its discovery was officially released to the world in 1956 when it was cut into separate strips at Manchester College of Technology in England. I would have to wait another four years until the text was finally published to read its breathtaking list of sacred wealth. I still wasn't sure exactly how I would keep that pledge I had made to my mother years ago, but I recognized the need to immerse myself in Hebrew if I was to accomplish some measure of success.

As a Baptist teacher trying to open up the scriptures to my own congregation I was troubled, not by the message of Jesus but the manner in which that message was handled. Translations from the Greek were problematic. I would encounter footnotes that revealed that a word or phrase was *"omitted in more ancient manuscripts."*

Who had decided to make an entry that the original authors decided not to include in the original text?

Even in my childhood, it was obvious to me that Jesus was a Jew. Your comprehension level would have to be very poor to miss that fact. I was also troubled by the schizophrenic character of some doctrinal issues regarding the Jews. Case in point is the narrative in Matthew wherein Jesus, himself a rabbi, made it very plain that he had no intention of undermining the authority of rabbis[1],

"The scribes and the Pharisees sit in Moses seat: All therefore whatsoever they bid you observe, that you observe and do."

This pronouncement is followed by a stinging reproach to those same teachers for being enormous hypocrites. But in the rush to condemn the scribes and Pharisees, most preachers eagerly ignore the fact that Jesus did not diminish the authority of those scribes and Pharisees.[2] In contemporary terms, he is reminding his disciples that when it comes to the rabbis, "Do as they say — don't do as they do."

I was also puzzled by the odd shift in tone in certain New Testament texts that gave them an anti-Jewish quality. For instance, I found that when the Greek word *sunagageh* was translated as "assembly," "congregation" or even "church," it was used in a favorable light. But when the translator wanted to offer a negative spin, the same Greek word was then rendered as "synagogue."[3]

I would later learn that traditional Judaism abhors those corrupt religious leaders such as Annas and Caiphas, who were appointed by the Romans. Many of my Christian friends would associate all of Israel and even modern Jews with those apostates of the Herodian era, painting even contemporary Jews with the same brush.

I simply did not know anything about the Jews. How was I supposed to keep faith with my own pledge made years ago if I ignored the very focus of that pledge? This drove me to my knees, asking G-d for the truth and pledging that if He would show me the truth, then I would accept and if I could understand it, I would teach it. Since Jesus was a rabbi who taught Torah, I went looking for a rabbi in October of 1956.

From this photo, one would assume that the more I struggled to gain wisdom, the faster my hair disappeared.

I called Rabbi Henry Gutman in Bristol, Virginia, informing him that I was with a church just over the mountain.

I didn't waste anytime sharing with him what was on my mind, "Rabbi, has Christianity changed since the time of Jesus? Why is there such a chasm between Jews and Christians. What's the problem?"

The pause on the other end of the line was prolonged. Maybe the rabbi had hung up on me.

"Are you still there," I asked.

He chuckled softly, "That's not exactly the kind of question that I expect from a Baptist minister. I can tell you that Judaism is only different today because we don't have the temple. Of course, we have just recently regained our land. I am sorry but I cannot tell you anything about Christianity."

I responded that Christianity had metamorphosed since its beginnings. And I understood that Constantine and the Council of Nicea were responsible for the anti-Jewish taint now present.

Gutman was duly intrigued. He invited me to come to his synagogue. I took up the challenge and decided to bring a Bishop with me, my friend Tom Bishop. We were warmly welcomed by the rabbi and his congregation. As the rabbi spoke, I began scribbling notes. An old gentleman next to me kindly informed me that they did not write on

Shabbat. After the service, the rabbi gave me a little tour of his synagogue. He showed me the *mikvah*, which I recognized from its Christian counterpart, the baptism.

The more I was exposed to this new world, the more I hungered for an explanation of its secrets. When I asked Rabbi Gutman if I could enroll in some kind of beginner's class, he informed me that his congregation was literally dying away. They were retirees and when their numbers dwindled to nothing, he would probably close the doors. But there was a Jewish day school in nearby Greenville, South Carolina.

I resolved to undertake a serious study of Judaism. If I were to do it properly it would mean starting my education in another town. I went home that night and told Lois that we had to move to Greenville. She was taken aback but didn't object. She had told me years ago that she would support my spiritual search wherever it took us.

Encouraged, I drove to meet with Rabbi Henry Barneis. It was a dreary overcast October afternoon when I arrived at his office to find the rabbi bent over his typewriter, tapping slowly at the keys. He listened attentively as I shared my thoughts about Judaism along with my desire to know more. I ended with a request to be schooled in the basics of Torah and Talmud. A deep frown creased the rabbi's brow.

He sat back from the typewriter and curtly responded, "I don't have time. If I had the time, I still wouldn't teach you. I have enough to do just teaching our Jewish community."

Without another word, he returned to his work.

I was shocked and embarrassed at his bluntness but managed to thank Barneis for his time. Stopping at his door, I paused to switch off the overhead lights. The startled rabbi looked up from his typewriter.

I stood there in the open doorway, "Rabbi, I didn't come here to teach you your scripture, but the prophet Isaiah says that Israel will be a light to nations. All I'm asking you to do is...."

I switched the light back on and made my exit.

As I walked back to my car, the Carolina skies hung overhead like a wet veil ready to suffocate me. Reaching for the car door, I heard Barneis behind me.

"Just a minute," he called to me, "Come back here!"

Back inside, seated in his office, the rabbi looked me over for a moment as if to reassess this odd young minister in front of him.

"When you walked into this office, you were a Baptist minister who wanted to study Judaism and who, for all I know would only learn Judaism so you could try to convert Jews to Christianity. If that were the case, I would not teach you. But you walked out as a Gentile wanting to learn Torah. What is your motive for wanting to learn Torah?" he asked.

I had to think for moment, "I can probably quote you any verse in the Old Testament but I have a sense that there is a vast difference between what those words mean to a Christian thinker and what they mean to a Jew who reads the same words. I just want to know Torah without it being sifted through Christian bifocals. I don't know anything about Torah but I do know that I am in love with the Author."

Rabbi Barneis managed a slight smile, "I will teach you. But first you must learn the Seven Laws of Noah. If you do well in that, we will see about going any further. My only stipulation is that you never raise questions about Jesus or the New Testament."

"It's a deal," I told Barneis, "you keep your knife in your pocket and I won't try to shove you in the water."

"What does that mean?"

"Rabbi, if you don't try to circumcise me, I won't try to baptize you!"

We both enjoyed a hearty laugh sealing what became a very lengthy association. For the next three and half years I studied with Rabbi Barneis until he moved to Ithaca, New York. It was then that I began an association with Rabbi Max Stauber of Spartanburg.

I am deeply indebted to Rabbi Barneis for introducing me to the riches of the Torah and Talmud; also to Rabbi Stauber for continuing to open my understanding while cultivating a lasting friendship. The ensuing years saw me investing much of my time and energy to everything Torah and Talmud. I would spend that time excavating the Bible. This sowed the seeds for a serious commitment to the deep truths that I was learning.

In my youth, I was indoctrinated by theologians who had discarded their Jewish brethren. They ignored a body of knowledge, backed up with thousands of years of study, by pious Jewish sages. These same theologians and pastors wanted the Jews to trade in their eternal Torah given to them by the Creator at Mount Sinai over three thousand years ago. They wanted the Jews to take that that profound manual of sacred instruction, written in Hebrew (the Mother of all languages and the very DNA of human speech,) and trade it in for a musty set of texts and doctrines cooked up in dank medieval monasteries. Later, I would realize that it took me seven years to learn Christian theology and fifteen years to unlearn it.

From 1964, I had lectured for the Biblical Research Society. Eventually my efforts gave birth to the Institute for Judaic-Christian Research (IJCR). Our mission statement, from the beginning, was to correct dangerous distortions and long-held misconceptions about Judaism, the Jewish People and the State of Israel. I wanted to create a bridge of understanding between Christians and Jews. Christians needed to recognize that many of their teachings came from a solid bedrock of Jewish principles — and that these principles were still relevant and timely for the Jews as they were thousands of years ago. By the same token, I wanted Jews to see that there were honest Christians who loved the God of Israel and recognized the simple but profound Bible fact: the Jews are the nation chosen by the Creator to be a Light Unto the Nations. A few years later, IJCR would become Vendyl Jones Research Institutes. It remains so to this day.

In all these years, I have never set out to convert anyone to Judaism not even my own children, even though two of them did convert and make *aliyah* to Israel. Conversion is a very personal decision and not to be taken lightly. However, for those who do not want to convert — but wish to follow G-d, Torah, and Israel — there is B'Nai Noach. It is not a new concept, nor is it a new religion. It is simply a template for living morally and ethically with one another.

Well, being seriously committed means that you either end up in an institute or you start one. I took the latter course so that I could develop more avenues of research and then distribute my studies in the form of articles, books and lectures. I also wanted an avenue to extend my research to the geography, geology and archaeology of the Bible and Israel.

The teaching is based on the seven ancient Universal Laws of Noah, taken directly from the Torah and recognized by all of the great Talmudic Sages. Before the revelation at Sinai, mankind was given these laws:

1. Against idolatry

2. Against blasphemy of G-d

3. Against murder

4. Against sexual perversion

5. Against theft

6. Against eating the limb of living animal

7. Establish Courts of Justice[4]

Notes

1 In the original Greek, Jesus is referred to as *rabbi* fourteen times but translators rendered the word as "master," however, *adoni* is the word meaning "master" or "lord."

2 Matthew 23:1-3

3 Compare Hebrews 10:25 with Revelations 3:9

4 I recommend *The Rainbow Covenant: Torah and the Seven Universal Laws*, by Michael Dallen, Lightcatcher Books, Springdale, AR.

A Closer Look at "3Q15"

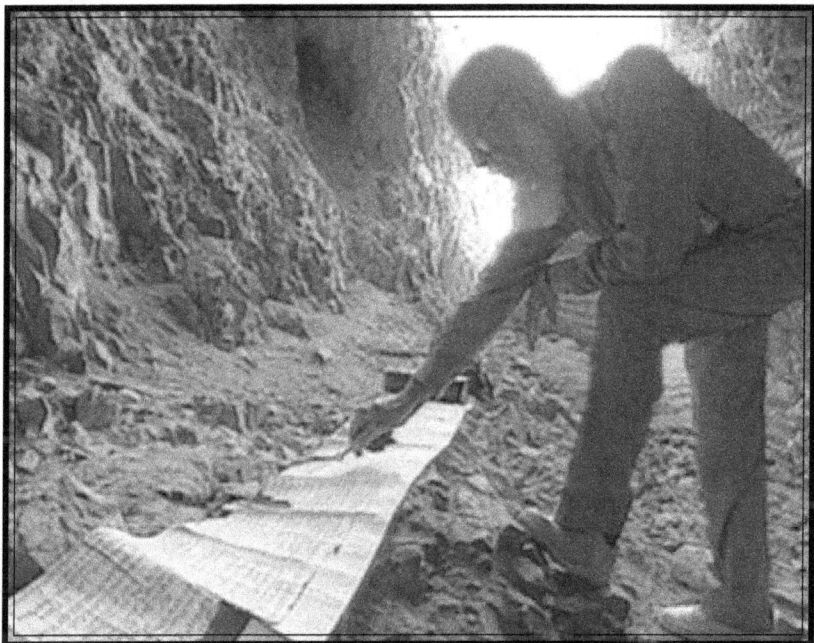

My continuing exposure to Torah and Talmud allowed me to grasp the nuances of the Hebrew employed in the Copper Scroll. It also deepened my understanding of those who wrote this document. The history and character of the Chosen People was being revealed to me in a way that I had never experienced.

After John Allegro and Father Josef Milik published their own translations of the Copper Scroll, I was able to secure a hand-drawn copy of the Copper Scroll text as it appeared hammered into the metal. I was finally able to conduct my own investigation into this wonderful document. There is so much that is unique about the Copper Scroll compared to the other scrolls found in the Judean wilderness in and around Qumran. It is so set apart in design, execution and content that it deserves a special status in the library of Qumran literature. Consider the following:

> ***It is the only scroll made of copper***
> ***ever discovered in Israel.***

One other copper scroll from antiquity was unearthed at Medinet Habu in Egypt.[1] The two coiled sections that were found in Cave 3Q were actually one long scroll about 8 feet in length. The copper was of the highest quality and nearly 1 millimeter thick. Since metal was of such purity, it was more malleable and therefore suitable for the inscribing text. Still, the words had to be hammered or punched into the surface with a stylus. This arduous method impacted the writing style of the Scroll.

> ***Unlike the other Qumran texts,***
> ***the Copper Scroll is not a book.***

Out of the approximately eight hundred scrolls found in the caves, the Copper Scroll is not a copy from one of the books found in the Biblical canon. It is not a narrative. It tells no story. It simply and concisely, in workman-like style, lists what most researchers believe are at least sixty-four hiding places for vast amounts of gold, silver and sacred artifacts secreted around the land of Israel. Accurate descriptions of the Scroll's text label the contents as dry and unimaginative — nothing like the colorful imagery in actual folklore. There's not even a plot. As you will see, there are actually closer to thirty-two hiding places, because the scroll lists the same burial places more than once.

*The Copper Scroll employs some symbols
which are definitely not Hebrew.*

In another chapter, I will address this curiosity at length. At this point, suffice it to say that these symbols have confounded most of the Scroll researchers. The non-Mishnaic symbols appear to be inventory marks, as stated in the end of Column 12.

The language of the Scroll is Mishnaic Hebrew.

The writings that form the Mishna are drawn from the oral and written Torah. Known as *halacha* (literally "the walk"), these laws were collected prior to Roman era and eventually redacted by Rabbi Yehudah HaNasi. This is important because the character of the language of the Mishna permeates the Copper Scroll, making it older than the other Qumran texts. Another vital clue gleaned from the language of the Copper Scroll demonstrates its parallel to the Zadokite Fragments. The Temple Scroll was also written in Mishnaic Hebrew in 3331 and is taken directly from the Mishnah. I believe the Mishnah was written by Joshua and the elders of Israel. Rabbi Akiva and Rabbi Yehuda HaNasi codified the Mishna into 63 Tractates. The un-codified Mishna fits letter on letter to the Temple Scroll. It is important to remember that the Copper Scroll is mentioned in the Temple Scroll found in Cave 11.[2]

*The paleography of the Copper Scroll
sets it apart from the other Qumran texts.*

Even to this day, there are several different translations
of the Copper Scroll. One reason is that the engraving mixes
square and cursive letters, and run-on words. It is sometimes
difficult to determine where one word ends and another
begins. Ancient Hebrew does not contain vowel points.
Modern Hebrew words carry these *nikodot* which tell the
reader which vowel sounds are used. Any variety of meanings
can be drawn from the ancient text. For example, in the last
few lines of the Scroll, on Column 12, most translations
reference a copy of the Scroll, but very few render this
intriguing phrase, "their oils," within those last few lines of
Hebrew, as found in the interpretation given by Al Wolters.[3]

*Inscribing the text onto the Copper Scroll must have been an arduous task.
This photo is actually of the replica produced by Electricitie de France.*

Granted, the Scroll is not the work of classical writers. Some of the Hebrew has confounded the experts. Possibly frustrated by the manner in which some of the letters are formed, these same experts have deemed the writing as the work of a semi-illiterate scribe.

> Odd — I wouldn't think that a semi-illiterate scribe could even get work. Would you dictate to, or allow a copy to be made, by someone who only possesses *half* the necessary skills to catalog your vast store of gold and silver?

More than one author inscribed the text
of the Copper Scroll.

Academicians fail to address the significance of this very obvious aspect of the Scroll text. Yet, it is pivotal to our investigation of the Scroll. As you will see, the classic *Emek Ha Melekh,* and the scrutiny of a handwriting analyst, make a solid case for multiple scribes.[4]

The fact the creators of the Copper Scroll used that metal for their valuable inventory is rare but not unusual in antiquity. A British metallurgist, Robert Feather, describes how the Harris Papyrus, housed in the British Museum, mentions copper plates. They were used for recording important data. In addition to extolling the achievements of Rameses III, the papyrus also lists his possessions. Among them are:

"...*tablets of copper in beaten work, a mixture of six [parts] of the color of gold, engraved and carved with a graver's tool with the great name of thy majesty, with the house regulations of the temples...*"[5]

Feather offers his own controversial theory for the origin of the treasures listed on the Copper Scroll found at Qumran. He believes the gold, silver and sacred objects come from the treasury of Akhenaton, the 18th Dynasty pharaoh famous for his heretical belief in only one deity. On this latter point, I respectfully disagree with Mr. Feather but do find some of his other theories about the Copper Scroll quite interesting. He is a metallurgist and that aspect of his research offers us some interesting insights into the provenance of the Copper Scroll.

Feather suggest that the unidentified symbols on the Copper Scroll are Egyptian numerical characters, used after the time of Pharaoh Akhenaten. This would place the origin of the Scroll squarely in the era of the First Temple. If anyone would question the use of Egyptian numerical symbols being used in a Hebrew Scroll, consider two possibilites:

1) Hebrew numerical equivalants are written with Hebrew letters — perhaps the scribes wanted to insure that certain deposits were not confused with a Hebrew word.

2) Israel, during the First Temple era, was influenced by Egyptian society, and made political alliances with their Southern neighbor. Even today, in Israel, numbers are not written in Hebrew.

Feather stresses that the Egyptian copper smelting process was quite sophisticated and their copper was known for its purity — a well-known feature of the Copper Scroll. Another interesting detail from Feather is a comparison of the Copper Scroll with one of the tablets referenced in the Harris Papyrus. He calculated that both segments were 99.9% copper with traces of arsenic and iron.

Close up of a segment of the CS. Note the severe deterioration of the metal,

Smelting and refining precious metals is exactly what took place as the Tribes of Israel encamped at Mount Sinai following their big exit from Egypt. It was during their year-long stay that they built the sacred treasures and the *Mishkan* (Tabernacle) to house them. These items were variously fashioned in gold, silver and copper. Not surprisingly, Feather confirms that:

"The logical place for learning such skills would be Egypt, as the Egyptians had an established tradition of advanced metallurgical knowledge."[6]

Like most scholars, Feather believes the quantity of gold and silver as listed in the Copper Scroll is problematic. According to his own research, if we were to use the generally accepted units of Biblical weights and measures, just the amount of gold would have represented a quarter of all the gold in the world at that time.

I must admit that when I first read Allegro's rendering of the Copper Scroll I was skeptical that it listed such vast amounts. But before we dismiss the idea that ancient Israel had access to such wealth, we should consider the Biblical and Talmudic records. Prior to the destruction of Jerusalem's *Beit Ha Mikdash* (Temple of Solomon) the treasuries of King Solomon were massive.

For instance, I Kings 10:14 relates that at one time Solomon received a shipment of over *six hundred talents of gold.*

A simple reading of the Bible's description of the amount of gold and silver Solomon used to beautify the Temple in Jerusalem will convince you that the wealth referenced in the Copper Scroll represents only a portion of the sacred riches. The chapter entitled *Emek Ha Melekh.* It describes how it was impossible to calculate the wealth that was in Jerusalem.[7]

Before we leave the subject of King Solomon, I want to make a very vital point regarding the Temple Treasures. Scholars err when they claim that much of Solomon's wealth, as well as items such as the Ark of the Covenant and comparable vessels, were carried off to Babylon. *This is a complete misreading of the Biblical text.* II Kings 24:13 does tell us that the Babylonians carried away those Temple vessels, *specifically made by Solomon.*

There is a clear distinction between those items manufactured under the authority of King Solomon and the most sacred vessels fashioned 480 years earlier at Mount Sinai.

These holiest of treasures had already been secreted away. Rabbi Shlomo Rotenberg, quoting the Talmud, reveals that in the 18th year of his reign, King Josiah, heeding the warnings of his prophet Jeremiah, sanctioned the removal of the Ark of the Covenant (containing the original Ten Commandment stones that were shattered by Moses) from the Holy of Holies. He told them to hide the Ark and also the container of Manna, the Anointing Oil, the Rod of Aaron, and the chest full of tribute from the Philistines.[8] Also hidden was the Breastplate of the *Kohan Gadol* (High Priest) embedded with twelve gemstones.

They remained concealed and were never used in the Second Temple. Of course, none of this will have any impact, if you view all of the above as folklore.

The Geography of the Scroll

According to the Copper Scroll, at Column 5, Line 12-14 and Column 6, Line 1, it says:

[5:12]   In the tomb which is in (at) the River of the Dome

[5:13]   in the coming (way) from Jericho to Succacah, dig 7 cubits, like this) {~squiggle sign~},

[6:1]   XXX (beside the ?) Cave of the Column with two openings

[6:2]   entrances viewing East

[6:3]   in the North opening viewing Eastward

[6:3]   in the hidden opening dig

[6:4]   3 cubits and there is the kalal

[6:5]   underneath it (the kalal) is one book [possibly the Silver Scroll]. To the East dig in the opening like this {~squiggle sign~}

[6:10]   7 cubits

[6:11]   in(side is the) complete Tabernacle on the side Westward. Dig Cubits

[6:13]   seventeen

[6:14-15] in the arch (which is the) chamber of the High Priest...

These seventeen lines contain and identify ten geographical and/or geological reference points. The "River of the Dome" is one of these. There are four rivers between Jericho and Succacah. Three of them are identified on current maps, one is not. From north to south, they include:

1) Wadi Kelt (also referred to as Ma'aleh Adummim, located just south of Jericho).

2) Wadi Hoglah (also referred to as Wadi Og, just south of Kibbutz Almog).

3) Wadi Nahal HaKippah (the third Wadi and the only one crested by a dome, runs on the north side of Kibbutz Qaliyah. This is Nahal HaKippah. The river has no modern map reference).

4) Wadi Qumran (the present-day name for this fourth is Wadi Qumran. Adam Smith, in his Smith Bible Dictionary written at the turn of the century, identified this wadi on modern maps of Israel as Wadi Qumran and also as Wadi Succacah.)

All of these wadis in 'Emeq-'Achor flow from the West to the East and each could provide an East/West map coordinate. The one, however, referenced here in the Scroll is the third Wadi called *"Nahal HaKippah."* It marks the proper East/West coordinate (See Column 5, Line 12, above). To pinpoint the location of the cave mentioned here in the Scroll, a North/South coordinate must be found to overlay against this East/West coordinate. The very next line in the Scroll identifies this North/South line as *"the [road] coming from Jericho to Succacah."*

The road from Jericho to Succacah runs from the North to the South and intersects the Wadi Nahal HaKippah as it runs from the East to the West. These geographical coordinates literally form an "X" which marks the spot! It is precisely at this intersection that we find the Cave of the Column. These descriptions and coordinates allow no other conclusion to be drawn from the geographical references in the Copper Scroll.

The Geology of the Cave of the Column

The physical description of the land can also be used to positively locate the areas referenced in the Copper Scroll. For example, the first column of the scroll reads:

[1:5]   Here is the Tabernacle, on the third level, and all the pieces of

[1:6]   gold. (squiggle) In the large hole that is in the court (large chamber) of the
[1:7]   pillar (column), deep in the wall that is covered (the) blue (which is)

[1:7]   opposite to the very high opening

1:9]   in the heap [Tel] (that is) blue....

The first mention of the Tabernacle is in Column 1, Line 5 of the Copper Scroll. This reference ties its location to the place discussed above in columns 5 and 6, but note that the corresponding description identifies the geology of the location rather than the geography.

Note, that Line 6 in Column 1 describes a very large hole that is high above the wall. It says there is a large hole in the upper chamber and that opposite the hole there is a hidden (or closed) opening. It also says that deep inside is something blue, although it does not say what. One more of the lines is the ninth which speaks of a heap or mound that is blue!

Notes
1 Robert Feather, *The Mystery of the Copper Scroll*, Bear & Company, Rochester, VT, 2003, p. 24.
2 See Table 6, p. 229, Vol. I of Yigal Yadin's *The Temple Scroll*, Institute of Archaeology, Hebrew University, Jerusalem, 1963.
3 Al Wolters, *The Copper Scroll: Overview, Text and Translation*, Sheffield Academic Press/Sheffield, England, 1996, p.55
4 See Chapter, *Making Dust*.
5 Feather, The Mystery of the Copper Scroll, p. 24.
6 Ibid, p.25
7 See Mishnah 11 of *Emek Ha Melekh*
8 Talmud, Horayot 12A, also see *Am Olam* by Rav Shlomo Rotenberg, Feldheim Publishers, Spring Valley, NY, 1988, p.108.

A Man of War

My philosophy began to change as I continued to study Torah. I was growing aware of a world that was much broader and richer than I had experienced in my previous studies of the Bible. World history no longer seemed to be a series of accidents, but more of a cyclical, elegant panorama.

History was prophecy.

The past is really a mirror image of the future. In fact the Hebrew word for a prophetic vision is *mar'eh* which can also be translated as "mirror," and is probably the source for our own English word "mirror". This can be demonstrated by examining the account of ancient Israel. The path trod by the Patriarchs became a pattern for their descendants, even impacting modern Israel.1

I expressed this concept by publishing a paper in 1959 entitled, *"Israel: Logical, Illogical or Eschatological?"*

The idea for the paper formed while reading Matthew in the Gospels. Eventually, I ended up in the Book of Daniel and the Torah. Using those sources, my ideas began to coalesce. What I found in the Book of Exodus was the key.

Boiled down to its essence, I saw a clear prophetical pattern for future the of Israel in the Creator's words as He instructs Moses to inform Pharaoh:

"God says, 'Israel is my son, my first born.'"[2]

The simplicity and the profound clarity of that statement opened up a window into the future. It would follow that, prophetically, Torah *mitzvoth* (commandments) that affected the first-born Jewish male applied to national Israel. I would soon witness this principle in action. Since modern Israel became a nation in 1948, it would be thirteen years old in 1961. Israel would somehow have a *Bar-Mitzvah.*

A Jewish male who reaches his thirteenth year is *Bar-Mitzvah* (literally, son of the commandment). He has reached the age of accountability and is considered a member of the community. If he breaks a Torah law, he must be judged by Torah law.

How did Israel experience its *Bar-Mitzvah?*

In 1961, Israel captured the infamous Nazi, Adolf Eichmann. Though he was responsible for the deaths of millions of Jews during the Holocaust, Israel managed to incur the wrath of much of the world. Even our own U.S. State Department criticized Israel for abducting him from Argentina (where he was hiding). They claimed that this act would have a profoundly negative impact on Israel's global relations.

Israel ignored the rants of much of the world body by citing an obscure legal concept called Universal Jurisdiction. Simply put, any sovereign state has the right to prosecute someone charged with war crimes — even heads of state. Those charged can be prosecuted without permission from any other sovereign state. No criminal is immune from prosecution.

Eichmann was tried and found guilty. His only defense for slaughtering millions of Jews was that he was just following orders.

Until Universal Jurisdiction was invoked by Israel, it had been all but forgotten.

Thus, Israel reached its *Bar-Mitzvah* year by affirming that criminals who ignore basic moral laws are to be held accountable. Israel stood for what was right, and demonstrated that it was a responsible member of the world community by this precedent-setting action. Ironically, the enemies of Israel have since attempted to cite Universal Jurisdiction by calling for the arrest and trial of Israeli Prime Minister Ariel Sharon for simply defending his country from the constant threat of terrorism.

I was beginning to see that the Torah concept of Israel as first-born might be tracked to their next experience. The next commandment that would signal a further growth of the son called Israel was as a Man of War. The Torah lists several passages where all males from twenty to fifty years of age were fit for combat as they emerged from Egypt — so they could "*go forth to war.*" [3] If this was correct, Israel would experience a major war as it was reaching its twentieth year in 1967, sometime between Passover and Shavuot.[4]

By the time 1967 arrived, I knew that I had to go to Israel. I could cite a number of concrete reasons:

1) to deepen my knowledge of Torah and the Prophets in a place that was teeming with the world's finest rabbinic scholars;

2) sharpen my Hebrew skills; and

3) I needed to get my feet on the same ground trod by
    these heroes to broaden my understanding of the
    actual physical lay of the land.

All of these elements would prove vital if I was ever to
unravel those Maccabean-referenced *"other records"* and locate
the treasures of the Copper Scroll. Any of those things would
have convinced those around me that I needed to go. Hardest
to explain was the profound and deep attraction that the land
of Israel exerted on me.

My plan was to enroll at Hebrew University and take
advantage of their Judaic Studies program. At the same time,
if I was wrong about my prediction of the coming war, it
might be better for all concerned if I left the country. But if
my theory was correct, then I would have a front row seat to
history!

Funding such a venture would not be easy. It may sound
cynical, but unless one plans to open a Bible college or start
some kind of missionary outreach, my Baptist contemporaries
were not interested. But a couple of miracles provided the
means for our passage to Israel.

I had been invited to give a series of lectures on the Book
of Daniel in and around rural Pennsylvania. Those talks raised
enough money for myself and my oldest, Wayne (*Gershom*),
to book passage. My last stop was a little Pentecostal
congregation where I was informed by the pastor that they

did not take an offering, but simply handed the speaker a check. I was fine with that and gave my talk.

After my teaching session, the pastor went to the front and informed his flock that my departure for the Promised Land was imminent, but that I would have to leave my family in the States. The pastor went on to say that he believed that they should do all they could to see that my family was kept together. They took a special offering that night and handed me nearly $20,000 dollars. Thanks to the unfailing kindness of such friends and supporters, Lois and I packed up the youngsters (Gershom, Sarah, Nunnery, Julie and Vinnie) and sailed out of New York toward the Middle East.

On April 10th, we entered the coastal waters of Israel. We stood there on the deck of the Queen Anna Maria, imbibing the beautiful vista before us. There was the port of Haifa, cradled in the shadow of Mount Carmel, where Elijah withstood the false prophets of Baal. Just to the north was another historic landing called Acco, one of the oldest cities in the world and a site that had witnessed some of the fiercest battles of the Crusades. Deeper into the interior and farther north, we could see the snows of Mount Hermon. I was overwhelmed, wanting to leap from the ship and kiss the shore. Here is the place that the Sages called the Center of the World, where the Creator chose to place his nation; a country where every ancient valley, hill and plain had been etched into my consciousness since childhood.

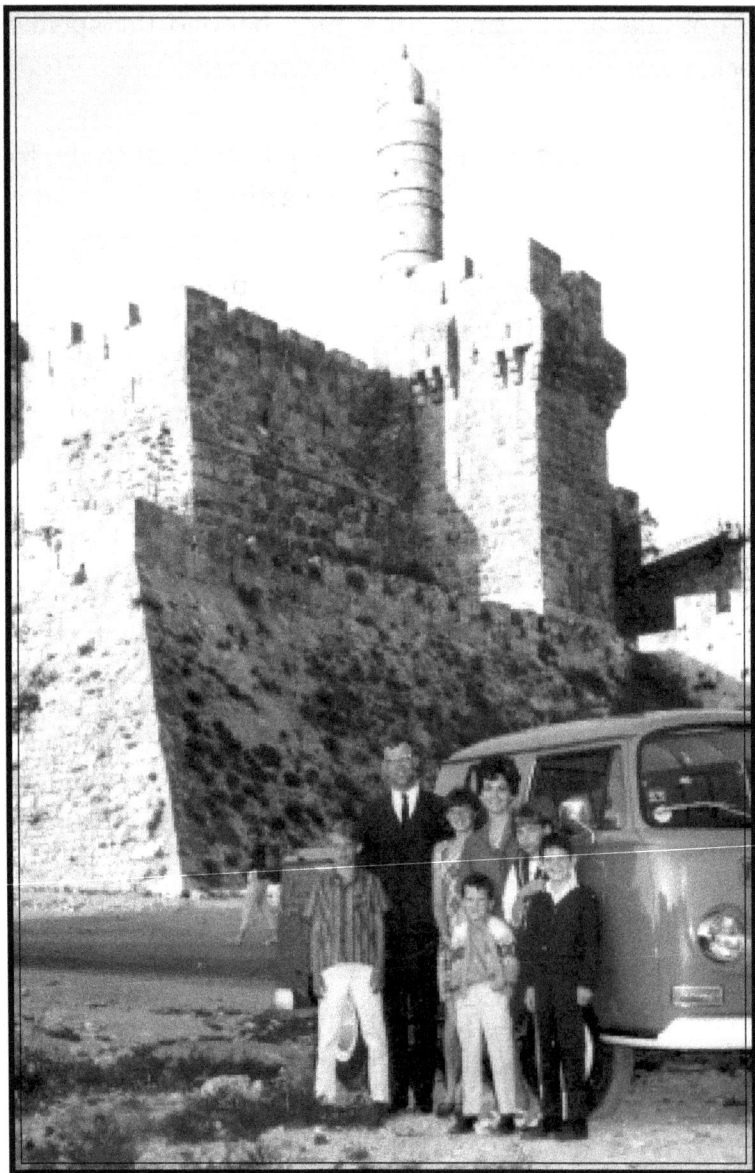

We arrived in Israel in April of 1967. That June we were witnesses to history during the Six Day War. Lois and I are with (left to right) Gershom, Sarah, Vinnie, Julie and Nunnery.

Just three days before our arrival, the Israelis, weary of the constant Syrian shelling of their villages in Galilee, retaliated with an air strike. The Syrians scrambled their Russian Mig-21's only to see six of the planes shot down by the Israelis in their French-made Mirage fighter jets. The Syrian skirmish was the flashpoint that Israel's enemies would fan into a full-blown war. Egyptian President Nasser would have to respond since he had signed a pact with the Syrians. But no believed that he would go to war.

We rented an apartment in Jerusalem at 50 Palmakh Street from Emmanuel and Lydia Ben Naeh. Lydia was from England, and he was a Jew of Persian birth. They were being sent to New York by the Jewish Agency. They were to set up educational programs to promote Israeli immigration. Their journey was delayed, so it was the seven of the Jones' clan and the three Ben Naeh's squeezed into the same living quarters.

At first, our choice of this quiet little neighborhood in Jerusalem didn't seem all that remarkable. I would quickly discover that we were within walking distance of two very remarkable men who would have a profound impact on my life. A half block from our house, at 54 Palmach Street lived an older gentleman who bore a very close resemblance to my father-in-law back in Texas. He strolled past our home one day and the children called my attention to the man who looked just like their grandfather.

I couldn't have picked a neighbor so utterly suited to introduce me to the mysteries of the Judean Wilderness. Bar-Adon had already made a name for himself discovering a mother load of artifacts in the Cave of Treasure. But the first time I saw him walk past the house, I had no clue that he was *the* Pesach Bar-Adon. It was not until after the war that I would finally meet him.

With the arrival of May, our clan was still sharing the house with the Ben Naeh family. Emmanuel continued to offer us advice on how to get things done the Israeli way, as we shopped at the grocery store called Super Sol, trying to fit in with the *sabras* and the *olim*.[5]

Though I had come from a Baptist background, the time spent with Rabbi Barneis and Rabbi Stauber had only whetted my appetite. I wasn't yet enrolled in my Judaic studies, so Emmanuel and I began a sort of Bible exchange study. Having spent much of his life in the Middle East, Emmanuel was unfamiliar with western religions. He wanted to get some of idea of what made a Christian tick and asked if I would explain New Testament basics. I agreed, if he would instruct me in Torah. One evening I decided to share my thesis about the coming war with him. He was an observant Jew and I felt he would appreciate my thoughts.

When I informed him that I believed that the war was about three weeks away, Emmanuel interrupted me, "You mean this *Lag B'Omer*?"[6]

"Yes," I replied.

"*Has v'Ha Lilah,* God forbid!" Emmanuel shook his head, "Wars don't happen that quickly. There is always a big buildup."

He leaned forward, "If Moshe Rebbenu (Moses) appeared to me and told me that there would be a war in Israel on *Lag B'Omer,* I would listen to him — but I wouldn't tell anyone!"

The following Friday night, with the arrival of Shabbat, Emmanuel and I walked to Beit Hillel Synagogue to hear Rabbi Jack Cohen teach. We strolled along the pavement basking in the sweet serenity that hovered over Jerusalem. Because it was Shabbat, no one was driving and a prayerful awe seemed to blanket the entire city. Not a car or bus could be heard. But that night, as we walked toward the synagogue, the roar of an army jeep pulled us from our reverie.

"What is this?" snapped Emmanuel. "They know they are forbidden to drive here on Shabbat!"

As the jeep sped away, we saw an approaching command car full of soldiers wearing *kippot.*[7]

"Oy," Emmanuel sighed, "there is something going on. There must be some kind of crisis, an alert. Those were religious guys...."

He trailed off and began reciting a Hebrew prayer under his breath.

We hurried on to the synagogue and found the meeting hall alive with tension. The President of Israel, Zalman Shazar entered and quickly strode to the bema, seating himself to the right of the Ark — the cabinet that housed the Torah Scroll. When the prayer was finished, Shazar addressed the congregation, gravely relating that the UN Peace Keepers were withdrawing from the Sinai and that Nasser had mobilized his eleven armored divisions. Shazar's voice became even more somber, telling us that the U.S. State Department would not intervene as stipulated in the Eisenhower-Dulles Agreement.

"Again," said Shazar, "we are left alone by our friends. But remember, Israel is not alone."

He turned and faced the Ark.

Soldiers began to file out of the synagogue. An army captain approached us and exchanged greetings with my friend. They consulted quietly for a few moments.

Emmanuel turned to me and said, "Vendyl, I am sorry. Can you find your way home?"

They whisked Emmanuel off to serve with *Zahal*, the Israeli Defense Forces, and I would not see him until the end of the Six Day War.

We braced ourselves in the days that followed. The reports of war grew with intensity. Surely, a full scale outbreak of hostilities would come without warning.

Each day the rumblings of war seemed louder. And then silence. Emmanuel's brother, David, decided to stop by for coffee.

Notes

1 The reader will find a good example of this by reading the account of Jacob's years of servitude to an idol-worshipping father-in-law. Jacob and his family grew. He finally departed taking great wealth with him. The 12 Tribes would collectively repeat this experience in Egypt.
2 Exodus 4: 22
3 See Numbers 1:3, also Numbers 26:2
4 The "Festival of Weeks" commemorates the 50th day of the Exodus when God gave the Torah to Israel at Mount Sinai.
5 A *sabra* is a native Israeli, named for the cactus plant that is prickly on the outside but sweet on the inside. *Olim*, are new immigrants. The word is a plural form of *oleh* which means to elevate or go up. A Jewish immigrant has made *aliyah* or literally "goes up" to the Land of Israel.
6 *Lag B'Omer* is the "counting of the omer" a Jewish festival held 33 days after Passover.
7 Plural for *kippah*, the knitted skullcap, also called a yarmulke, worn by observant Jews.

In the Presence of a Prophet

"What do you think, Vendyl? Nasser has grown quiet. A lot of people say he's changed his mind. Do you think there will still be a war?" David asked.

I confidently said, "You know, I'm from Texas and I've seen plenty of tornadoes. Just before one of 'em drops out of the cloud, it's preceded by a deadly silence. I think that's just where we are now."

"Emmanuel told me what you said about the war. I want you to show me how you knew that," he stated.

"It could take me at least four or five hours to explain it. It might be kind of complicated," I replied.

"I have five hours," he responded.

It was well after midnight when I finished. David sat back in his chair eyeing me for a few moments.

"There is a holy man who lives in Safed who, like you, predicted many years ago that there would be a war in 1967. His name is Rabbi Chaim Shvili. I will go to the Ministry of Religious Affairs and get his address. You must meet him," David said.

Sunday morning came with an enthusiastic knock on my door. It was David Ben Naeh.

He shook his head and chuckled, "Come with me, I want to show you something."

We walked out into the yard and David pointed at the intersection.

"Chaim Shvili has moved from Safed to Jerusalem. You could throw a stone and hit his house from where we are right now! Maybe God wants the two of you to meet," he said.

David led me down the street, walking quickly to the door and knocked.

Our first home in Israel at 50 Palmach Street. We were within walking distance of an eminent archaelogist and a saintly seer. (VJRI photo)

We were greeted by an old gentleman whose face was not weathered, but graced by the years. Though he was quite advanced in age, his eyes were bright — almost blazing. I had never seen eyes like that in my life. His house was sparse and austere. The only ornate things in his home were his books. But these volumes were not used for decoration. They were musty with age and well-used. Several of the heavy bound editions were held together with twine to keep them from falling apart. But nothing could detract from the *neshama* (spirit) that filled the house.

We were in the presence of a holy man.

Rabbi Shvili invited us to join him around the table. David could not contain his enthusiasm and before he was seated began to pour out what I had shared with him concerning the coming war. But the rabbi seemed unmoved. He simply listened until David had finished.

Shvili was of Lithuanian descent, but like those educated in Israel during the British Mandate, he sounded like someone who had grown up in London.

He spoke to me in a low-pitched resonant tone, "You are knowledgeable in the Book of Daniel?"

"Uh... I am a student of Daniel. I am not a scholar, but yes, I have studied the Book of Daniel," I replied.

"Do you know how many visions Daniel saw or how many he interpreted?" he asked.

"Seven," I replied.

Shvili nodded, "Do you know the theme of each vision?"

As soon as I named them, Shvili pressed me again asking, "How do each of the visions of Daniel relate to each other and how do they relate to time and history?"

I began to expound on my studies in the Book of Daniel, droning on with no thought of the time. When I had finished, Rabbi Shvili turned to David and they quietly conversed in Hebrew. At one point, it occurred to me that I was breathing the same air as this man. I wondered if he would ever consent to teach me. I braced myself and decided to ask him if I could become his student.

"I won't teach you," he smiled, "but I will study with you."

David took me back to that little house many times. I would sit at this sage's feet learning the mysteries of *Kabbalah*. Rabbi Chaim Shvili was from the school of Rabbi Luria of Safed. This sage, known as the Ari, stressed *Tikkun Ha Olam*, the repairing of the world. Luria was versed in *Gematria*, *Atbash* and other coded forms of revelation. Luria's students approached the Torah text in an almost scientific methodology rather than meditating as some practitioners.

I want to digress briefly, to make it clear that this was genuine *Kabbalah*. It is nothing like the New Age pap being fed to Madonna and her friends. Nor is it some dark creed thick with voodoo or incantations. *Kaballah* means literally "that which is received." It is the deeply mystical teachings taken directly from the words of Torah and transmitted by the Sages. It is the soul of the Torah. Some of Judaism's greatest scholars were schooled in *Kabbalah* and many were known for their kindness and their deep love of God. The Biblical patriarch, Abraham — a figure considered to be the epitome of faith and loving-kindness — was said to be a *kabbalist*.

In 1922, Rabbi Shvili had published *The Time of the Sons of Amelek Has Come.*

It was a prophetic cry to the Jews of Europe that they should flee to Palestine and escape the coming slaughter. In it Shvili wrote:

> *"Each day you remain in Europe, it will become more difficult to leave. Not only that, but each day entering Palestine will become more difficult."*

Shvili possessed the knowledge, referenced in I Chronicles 12:33, of the tribe of Issachar, who were "men of understanding of the times to know what Israel ought to do."

One of the ways he understood the times was to translate the Hebrew year into a word or phrase. For example, 1973 was 5734 on the Jewish calendar. Since there are no numerical characters in Hebrew, the letters carry values. The year 5734 was written *tav-shin-lamed-dalet*. It also contains the word, *sheled* which means "skeleton."

With a deeply troubled look, Rabbi Shvili revealed this to me, "Many brave Jews will die that year."

He was right. It was the year of the disastrous Yom Kippur War that saw the Arab armies inflicting heavy casualties — many of them in the first month of fighting. Moshe Dayan would record later in his memoirs that the Yom Kippur was different from the previous wars fought by Israel. Ultimately, the meaning of that war held more tragedy for Rabbi Shvili. The first week of fighting, he lost a son in the Sinai.

Seven days later, coming home from the funeral, he was informed that his other son had fallen in battle. Yet their grief would multiply even more as they returned from the double mourning to be informed that his third son had perished fighting in the Golan Heights. It was more than this precious saint could bear. All three of his beloved sons had died. He went to be with them and passed on. In November of 1990, the Associated Press would tell the world of Shvili when it wrote, "...*in 1935 a seer predicted the use of chemical and germ warfare in the 1990's.*"

Sometimes, deep in the night when I am pondering a Torah passage or gazing at the words of the Prophets, I sense him in the room and feel the sweep of a peaceful presence that embraced us as we sat in Shvili's library in the Jerusalem of 1967.

Milchamah

On a Sunday morning, the news came that King Hussein of Jordan had met with Egypt's Nasser on the past Friday. He had committed his army to the effort, and Syria had joined the fray. The most serious development was that Russian officers were replacing Arab commanders. Israel was on the brink of war. I held on to my belief that war would come. That conviction led me to volunteer for combat service in the Israeli Army. They wouldn't accept me, telling me that they could not endanger the lives of American civilians. An offer to drive an ambulance met the same resistance.

Later I heard a broadcast report from Kol Israel Radio that the government needed volunteers to aid in the harvest in the Negev. I had made the wheat harvest from Texas to Canada for three seasons and figured that if I couldn't fight, then I would lend civilian support. I caught a bus to Kibbutz Maale Hachamisha, located just a few miles north of Jerusalem on the way to Tel Aviv.

Thanks to a vast irrigation project called the Israeli National Water Carrier, the country had reclaimed thousands of acres of harsh desert land. Their fields were flourishing.

The Kibbutz owned farm land in the Negev and needed combine drivers. I don't know if it was my Texas accent, but I convinced them that I was their man. I was loaded onto a truck the next morning and transported to their wheat fields near the Egyptian border.

Nothing could have prepared me for cutting wheat on a John Deere combine in Israel. The stalks were the largest I had ever seen. I spent much of my time, adjusting the cylinder on my machine to accommodate the massive stalks. We were reaping over 800 kilos of wheat per acre. I spent all of May, and even my birthday, harvesting wheat for Israel. We didn't stop until June 5th.

In a brilliant pre-emptive strike, early that morning, a single Israeli squadron, flying low enough to elude radar and close enough to use hand signals, had crippled several major Egyptian airfields. The Six Day War had begun.

That morning, with the very real threat of facing a horde of Egyptians, we decided to return to Kibbutz Maale Hachamisha. Within a few hours we had made our way into the hills north of Jerusalem, just minutes from the Kibbutz. We were riding in a one-and-half-ton transport with a canvas top over the beds. I was sitting in the cab on the passenger side, as the truck maneuvered through the steep, hilly terrain near *Kiryat Yearim*. Lost in thought, I scanned the topography recalling the story of how King David had come this way, bringing the Ark of the Covenant back to Jerusalem.

I snapped back to reality when the surface of the road exploded sharply with blasts from a machine gun. We were taking fire from an Arab bunker somewhere above us. The truck in front of us wheeled crazily, the front whipping around. We could see the shattered, blood stained windshield and behind it, the driver slumped lifelessly behind the wheel.

Our own driver managed to brake quickly, and we scrambled from the cab of the truck. I tumbled into a nearby ditch where I was soon joined by two screaming women. They had been behind our vehicle, and when the bullets began to rain down, they had abandoned their car for the safety of the ditch. Panic and confusion mingled with gunfire until we felt the air move from the concussion of a shell hitting nearby. The Israelis had already targeted the enemy position and were pounding it with mortar rounds. It was all over in two minutes. I heard a voice behind me, and turned to see an Israeli soldier coming out of the trees announcing almost casually, "*Kol B'seder*" ('everything is okay')."

Shaken, but thanking God for our survival, we made our way back to Kibbutz Maale Hachamisha. It was only six miles from Jerusalem and as we approached we could hear the constant report of gunfire and shelling. We found the Kibbutz alive with volunteers preparing for battle. They had gotten word that the nearby orchards were thick with possibly eighty Egyptian commandos. This was the same squad that had attacked us on the road to the Kibbutz.

When I saw a group of men queuing up to receive their weapons, I fell in line. I took a rifle, and I fell out, ready for action. I felt a hand on my shirt collar. My rush to join the ranks of civilian fighters was over before it began. I spun around and recognized the shock of white hair and sunburnt face of Abraham, an older Kibbutz member.

He snatched the weapon from me and growled, "You don't need that!"

"Well, I'm not sittin' around here so I can wait to get shot. I've got family back in Jerusalem," I responded and turned to leave the grounds of the kibbutz.

Abraham was right behind me and grabbed me again.

"If you go down that road the Jordanians will shoot you within ten paces!" he snapped.

I pulled myself from his grasp and straightened my shirt.

"I know better than that. I'm heading back to Jerusalem through the Sorek Valley," I explained.

Abraham shook his head saying, "That's worse. Then the Israelis will shoot you! You can't go anywhere right now. And I can't give you a weapon without permission."

With that, he returned to main hall of the camp, leaving me to ponder my fate.

I wandered back to a basement bunker for a cup of coffee, and found a volunteer examining an old German machine-gun with a belt feed. I don't recall the gentleman's name, but I do remember him telling me that he'd made *aliyah* over twenty years ago from Los Angeles. He had come to Israel to die, and twenty years later he was still alive. I noted that he was puzzling over the mechanics of the weapon.

"Do you know how to handle one of these?" he asked

I looked over the gun and found it was very much like a Browning Automatic Rifle, the only difference being that the breach went the opposite direction. I fed the ammo belt in, slapped the breech shut and pulled the cocking mechanism back.

"Yeah, I think I could operate this," I said, tapping the muzzle.

We looked up to see Abraham enter the bunker. Seeing me, his face collapsed into a frown. He shook his head as if to say, "Not you again!"

The elderly ex-Angelino pointed at me and suggested, "Look Abraham, I found someone who can operate the machine gun."

Abraham eyed the cocked weapon and gave me the once-over.

"If I get you permission to use this gun, will you follow my orders?" he asked.

"Just get me permission," I grinned.

"I don't know if I can actually get you permission. And I can't tell you to fire that weapon — but I cannot stop you from defending yourself."

He motioned to the canisters of ammunition stacked next to the rifle.

"You can use all of this against the Egyptians," he said as he pointed to one ammo box marked in red, "but do not touch this box!"

With that he left the bunker.

The old gentleman had gone with Abraham so I was alone in the bunker. What was with this guy, I thought. Glancing at the special canister, I gave in to my curiosity and unlatched the top. Inside were several ammo belts exactly like the others.

Abraham returned with a sidearm, a helmet, and permission.

I motioned toward the specially marked ammo box, "I don't understand why I can't use this. It's no different than the rest."

Abraham was silent for a moment as he stared at the box. He lifted his gaze and locked eyes with me.

He spoke evenly, his words tinged with sadness, "Now listen to me. If the commandos come through that orchard, we will send the women and children down here with you. If, God forbid, you should run out of ammunition and the Egyptians are still advancing, then…" he pointed to the marked ammo box, "you are to use this box of ammo to kill our women and children."

The room around me seemed suddenly darker. The blood in my head pounded a little louder while a deep place in the pit of stomach knotted into a tight coil.

"Why in the name of God would I do that?" I blurted out.

He quietly responded, "You wouldn't ask that if you had seen what they did to the innocent people of Hebron in 1929. A wild Arab mob attacked their Jewish neighbors with knives and hatchets. They butchered *yeshiva* students. Some of them raped our women then cut off their breasts. They hacked off the limbs of children and cut open pregnant women. If they attack us, the Egyptians will carry out the same kind of atrocities."[1]

I could not respond. It was one thing to shoot an enemy combatant that is screaming for your blood. But to turn a machine gun into a crowd of women and children who have counted on you to save their lives....

"Can I count on you to follow that order?" he demanded.

I shook my head and stammered, "Abraham, I...."

He pounded on the ammo box insisting, "I want to know if I can count on you to do this, if necessary!"

A thick growing dread caught in my throat and I choked out a question, "Is this Auschwitz or Masada?"

"It's Masada!" he shouted.

"Then I can do it," I affirmed.

Thank God, I never had to make that decision because the *kibbutznik* whose job it was to man that automatic weapon walked into the bunker a few minutes later. And the Egyptian commandos never materialized in the orchards. At this point, I felt that I couldn't do much for the war effort sitting around the Kibbutz. I was dismissed from my post — but I still had my helmet, gun and permission to use it. I quickly made my departure and headed north for the front which was only a few minutes away by foot. The corridor that led to Jerusalem was the old 1949 Armistice Line — and that day it was the Jordanian Front. The Kibbutz was being fired on by the enemy from a site across the valley known as Radar Hill. But the valley below the Kibbutz was infested with enemy troops.

The Israeli position was a trench being manned by a young officer named David Warhowski. He didn't quite know what to make of me.

"Who sent you?" he asked.

I jabbed a thumb in the air back toward the Kibbutz and fibbed, "They sent me. I've been on guard duty. I have permission," I added, hoping to enhance my credibility.

He didn't seem all that sure about allowing this stranger to man one of his guns, so David handed me a pair of binoculars.

"I want you to keep an eye toward *Bidu*, down in the valley and also watch the road to Tel Aviv," he said.

I am color-blind, and have been since I was a youngster. I think the disorder may have come from gazing too long at the sun one afternoon. It had damaged a vital bundle of cone-shaped nerves that allowed me to distinguish between red and green.

I scanned the no-man's-land which, according to what we would call rules of engagement, should have been empty. No one told the Jordanians that we were supposed to fight like gentleman. My visual disorder turned out to be an enormous blessing that summer day in Israel. As I scanned the thick undergrowth below me, I caught a glint of something shiny. It was the dye used to mimic nature's colors in the Jordanian camouflage. It shone like new money. I put the field glasses down. Even without them, I could see a Jordanian position that was not supposed to be in the valley. When I pointed out the bunkers, David shook his head.

He said, "There's nothing there, Vendyl."

I walked over to a large machine gun and pointed into the valley. I peered through the sights of the weapon. Just barely I could make out three Jordanian soldiers. One was wearing the familiar red-checkered *kafiyah*. I locked the gun in place and called David over.

He squinted into the sights and gasped, "I don't believe it!"

Immediately he ran to a field telephone and called in the coordinates of the bunkers. The response was instant, and the Israelis rained down fire on the unsuspecting Jordanians. Before the day was out, I had located sixty-six anti-tank positions and four personnel bunkers in the valley below us.

It was also the day that I permanently damaged my hearing. An Israeli tank rolled up to our position and they shouted a command in Hebrew to clear the area. But I didn't understand the warning. The tank fired. The ensuing concussion sent huge clouds of dust, heavy rocks, and a young Texan tumbling across the ground. I was convinced that we'd been hit by incoming shell fire and jumped up to get out of the trench. That's when the tank fired a second time,

Though taken years later, this shot is reminiscent of my experiences during the Six Day War.

knocking me down again. Completely disoriented, I managed to crawl out of the trench and away from the tank before another round was fired — but the damage was done.

Later in the day, Brigadier-General Uzi Narkiss came to our trench.

Narkiss hailed me, "Shalom!"

"Shalom? How about *Milchamah* (war)!" I responded.

He laughed and took my hand and said, "I wasn't giving you a report but a prayer."

He pumped my hand energetically and uttered, "Mr. Jones, there is no telling how many Israeli lives that you saved today."

Narkiss had seven brigades under his command. He would make history two days later by leading the offensive that liberated the Old City, allowing Jews to pray at the *Kotel* (Wailing Wall) for the first time since 1948. That victory has been forever memorialized in a famous photograph that shows Narkiss entering the Lion's Gate with Moshe Dayan and Itzhak Rabin.

Before the sun set, we witnessed some of the fiercest fighting of the war, as the Israelis re-took the heavily fortified Radar Hill. Brave Israeli boys picked their way through mine fields, some losing limbs. At one point, they engaged the Jordanians in close quarter hand-to-hand combat.

That night, exhausted but exhilarated, I silently thanked God for allowing me to witness history unfold and being a part of it. In some small way, I felt that I was able to finally respond to the call that I felt so many years ago in that small town theater, helplessly watching the brutal images of death camps.

Notes
1 The Hebron Massacre of 1929 is a well documented atrocity that left 67 Jews dead, and numerous others permanently mutilated. Today, in the heart of Hebron, there is a museum displaying graphic images of the aftermath.

The Valley of Achor

"And I will give her vineyards from there, and the valley of Achor for a door of hope; and she shall sing there, as in the days of her youth, and as in the day when she came out of the land of Egypt." - Hosea 2:17

The smoke and fire of battle had barely subsided when I hitched a ride on a meat truck bound for Jerusalem. I was dropped off near the Temple Mount and found the streets empty and silent as a prayer. Before I walked much farther a screeching trill of staccato blasts cut the air. It was a *shofar* being blown from the *Kotel* (Western Wall). As the ram's horn echoed across the hills of Jerusalem an exhilarating sensation gripped me. It is a moment fixed in my memory. That sound told me that the Holy City was liberated and the Western Wall was in Israeli hands. Years later I would meet the extraordinary man who had sounded the *shofar*.

When I finally returned to Palmach Street I discovered that Lois and the children had spent most of the Six Day War in and out of a basement, at the Super Sol grocery store, that served as bomb shelter. I was caked in dirt and sweat, so much that they didn't even recognize me when I arrived home.

Showered and refreshed, I sat down to mentally regroup from the events of the past few days when I heard a loud knock at my front door. It was my neighbor, Yakov

Yaphet. He was a major in the Zahal stationed down at Jericho when he heard of my contribution to the war effort. I opened the door to a bottle of Johnny Walker being brandished in my face.

"Vendyl, you have done a wonderful thing and everyone's talking about you. It's all over the radio about the Baptist from Texas, even the military radio!" he exclaimed.

That was thrilling to hear. I would later learn that *Time Magazine* even made mention of my experience in their June 16th issue, though I cringed at being dubbed "Reverend Jones."[1]

Yakov pulled up a chair at our dining table and asked for two glasses. He opened the bottle.

Smiling broadly at me he offered, "Vendyl, we're going to make a L'Chaim!"

No liquor had passed over my Baptist lips for almost twenty years. Despite my objections, Lois produced two glasses from the cabinet.

"Vendyl, you're being a poor host," she warned, "make a L'Chaim."

Yakov splashed two fingers of the whiskey into the glasses. We clinked them together. He tossed his drink back while I sipped on mine. When he offered me another shot I declined, still getting used to the sharp snap of the whiskey against the back of my throat.

Yakov poured another drink, "My daughter, Yael, said that your little girl told her that you want to go to Qumran."

"Yakov, as soon as the roads are open, I want to go."

He looked over his glass at me and tipped the bottle over my glass again.

"Mr. Jones," he said in measured tones, "Every road in Israel is open to you."

It was 4:00 am the next morning when we loaded our provisions into Yakov's jeep and began the roughly twenty-five mile drive from Jerusalem to the Dead Sea. Gravity took over as we sped along pushing quickly down a twisting asphalt ribbon that cut through deep narrow passes. The highway followed a meandering corridor that led to the lowest place on the face of the earth, the Dead Sea Valley. At its lowest point it is over 1,300 feet below sea level. The jeep rounded a crag and the valley floor suddenly opened up and spread out below us into a vast plain. We were now heading due east. The sun was just breaking over the ancient mountains of Moab in Jordan. We could just discern the northern end of the Dead Sea in the morning haze.

Looking behind the jeep I noticed how sharply the Judean hills fell away, becoming a distant, lofty line of cliffs behind us. We passed a slender marker on the left that pointed north to Jericho. The weathered concrete post boasted, "Jericho: Oldest City in the World." All around us were low, scrubby hills creased with a hundreds of dry ravines called *wadis*.

I noticed the increase in temperature as the wind warmed my face, and I thought we would run out of road as the nearly motionless waters of the Dead Sea began to loom ahead. But directly in our path was a small unadorned block building. Yacov pulled the jeep into the front of the structure.

He said, "C'mon Jones, it's time for breakfast. I'm buying."

We were greeted warmly by a young Arab wearing a linen *galibeyah*. After seating us, he promptly brought out a pot of hot Bedouin coffee flavored with a hint of cardoman. That was followed by a stack of pita, hummus, and fresh vegetables with a dry white cheese. I felt like I hadn't eaten in weeks. I couldn't get enough.

After breakfast, we headed south, past rows of date palms. Within minutes we pulled up the sharp incline to the ruins of *Qumran*. I would later learn from my Bedouin friend, *Musa*, the name of the region meant "two moons." It was derived from an Arab root word *qamar* meaning "moon." At certain times when the winds subsided after sunset, the still, glassy surface of the Dead Sea would offer an eerily perfect reflection of the full moon. One would see two moons.

Not surprisingly, there was a rusty iron gate blocking the entrance. Yakov remarked that there should have been a guard on duty. But he dismissed this with a wave and handed me a packed lunch and a canteen.

"You will need these, Vendyl. Be sure you drink plenty of water. Wander to your heart's content — but meet me right here at five o'clock," he requested.

He jammed the jeep into gear, backed down the hill speeding north back to Jericho.

I wandered around the ruins, picking my way around the piles of stones and examining the walls, noting that some had been recently reconstructed. I thought that I was alone until my attention was drawn to the sound of a shovel striking dirt. It was coming from the southern part of the ruins.

I headed in that direction and spotted two men. At first glance they both appeared to be Bedouin. The one watching the other dig was a slender, shirtless man wearing a *kafiyah* on his head. It occurred to me that one of them might be the guard. They were hunched over a shallow depression, surrounded by piles of stones. As I approached, the shirtless man did his best to ignore me.

"Howdy, I'm Vendyl Jones," I said.

A short, hawk-nosed man turned abruptly to me, pulling down a scarf that covered his mouth.

"Howdy?" He stood up and looked at me, and said with relief, "you're not an Israeli."

I stuck out my hand and grinned, "Vendyl Jones, from Texas."

He flicked bits of dust from his fingers and shook my hand, "Solly Steckoll."

"I don't mean to pry but is it okay for you to be digging here or are you taking advantage of the war?" I asked.

Without a word, he reached into a canvas bag and produced a couple of documents, shielded in plastic. One was written in English and the other in Arabic. They were both stamped with the royal seal of the King of Jordan. Steckholl proudly tapped the seal, "I have permission from his majesty, King Hussein, himself."

Solomon H. Steckoll was a curiosity to me. He was an Israeli citizen, until he witnessed the infamous *Altalena* Affair in June of 1948. It is one of the darker chapters in the history of modern Israel. What began as a power struggle between two factions of Israelis (the Irgun and the new provisional government of David Ben-Gurion,) escalated into the shelling of the *Altalena*, a ship bringing a cargo of arms to Israel for Menachem Begin. The action led to the tragic deaths of Israelis at the hands of their own countrymen. Steckoll was so discouraged that he left Israel and became a citizen of Canada. There he produced a series of articles so critical of Ben-Gurion that he drew the attention of King

Hussein of Jordan. Hussein admired the screeds so much that he would issue Steckoll a permit to dig at Qumran.

During our first meeting among the ancient graves at Qumran, he motioned toward mounds of rocks surrounding us and said, "Roland de Vaux thinks that Qumran was the start of Christianity. He believes this was a community of celibate priests – the monks that supposedly lived here didn't allow any females on the compound. I'm going to prove he's wrong. I believe I already have. There are graves that contain the remains of women who lived and died here at Qumran. I know there are more."

"How'd you like some help?" I asked.

Standing at the Cave of the Column looking south; in the distance, the ruins of Qumran and beyond that the Dead Sea

Steckoll smiled broadly at me, "I'd like that very much."

I rolled up my sleeves and joined him. It was my first dig in Israel. That decision turned out to be a double-edged sword that would later hinder and help me in Israel. I assisted him in excavating nine of the graves. He would eventually uncover the remains of six men, two women and an infant. It's interesting to note that one of the women had been pregnant when she died.

Steckoll's findings and his conclusions were met with scorn. Some of the Scroll scholars rejected his work outright on the basis that he was not an archaeologist, despite the solid analysis done by two doctors, Haas and Nathan, who served as forensics experts on the team. Steckoll's academic foes spared no ink in their efforts to ridicule him. Leading the attack was Father Roland de Vaux who challenged the authorities to rid the site of Steckoll, mocking him as the "Sherlock Holmes of Qumran."

I worked with Solly Steckoll from June 5th until the end of January. Though we became friendly, I could see how his radical reputation was well-deserved. He was a world-class rascal, an iconoclast whose religious beliefs bordered on the pagan. The skeletons that we exhumed were thousands of years old, and I believed that remains of the dead should eventually be returned to the earth. But Steckoll had an inkwell made from one of the bones.

Though he had his critics, I will never forget the kindness that Solly displayed when my thirteen-year-old son Gershom suffered from serious renal failure and required a kidney transplant. We needed money for airfare to fly myself and Gershom to see a specialist in Houston.

Steckoll had recently published *The Gates of Jerusalem*, a thoughtful tour through the Holy City's numerous and ancient gates augmented with striking photography by Dalia Amotz. Steckoll had just received some proceeds from the book's sale, and when he learned of our predicament, promptly signed the check over to us. The amount was exactly what we needed for the airfare. Later, when I attempted to repay Solly, he wouldn't hear of it. Gershom endured fifty surgeries and two complete transplants before making a full recovery.

During this same period that I met Steckoll, I forged my friendship with Pesach Bar-Adon. Like many others, Pesach had an enormous impact on my life. He had already made a place for himself in the annals of archaeology when he discovered a cache of antiquities in the cliffs south of Ein Gedi, along the shores of the Dead Sea. Known now as the Cave of Treasure, the site yielded a depository of 429 artifacts — mostly made of copper. Among these fascinating objects were tools, some weapons and even curiously made crowns.

I finally met Pesach while driving down King David Street in Jerusalem one afternoon in April of 1968. I was passing the historic King David Hotel on my left and glanced to the opposite side of the street to see a familiar face. Strolling in front of the Jerusalem YMCA, was the neighbor who resembled my father-in-law back in Texas.

I wheeled the van over to the curb and hailed him, "Say pardner, can I give you ride?"

Pesach pulled a pipe from his mouth and approached the van, "I am sorry. Do we know each other?"

I offered my hand, "I'm your neighbor on Palmach Street, Vendyl Jones."

Pesach's eyes grew large, "You! You are Jones the Baptist!" he shouted.

The van door flew open and the old gentleman jumped in, slid across the seat and hugged me, "Welcome to Israel! You have done a wonderful thing! Wonderful!"

I pulled away from him, amused but appreciative of his enthusiasm, "No, please. I just did what I could. I'm just glad to be here. It's such an exciting time."

I shifted the van into gear and drove on. As we talked about the war and the many changes it brought.

Pesach invited me to his house for coffee.

"Sure, can I bring my wife?" I asked.

"Well, you can bring your wife, but my wife died fifteen years ago, and my house has not been cleaned since." he replied.

"Okay, then you come to my house for supper," I smiled.

As he accepted, I realized that I had forgotten to ask his name.

"I am Pesach Bar Adon," he replied.

Now it was my turn to hug him as I exclaimed, "Are you the archaeologist? I cannot believe this! I have read all about your work in the Judean Desert. I cannot tell you how much I admire your work. Bring your maps!"

For my money, this Polish immigrant with the deep sun-beaten tan had done a masterful study along the shores of the Dead Sea. He had roamed the forgotten hills and cliffs, identifying nearly every *wadi* and path in that region.

That night would be the first of many that Pesach would join us around the supper table. We cleared the dishes after our meal, and while Lois made coffee, Pesach spread a wealth of charts and maps across the tabletop.

As I scanned the material, I asked him, "Pesach have you located *Nahal Ha Kippah* (River of the Dome)?"

"Ah, you have been reading the Copper Scroll," he shot me a quizzical look, "we would all like to know where is *Nahal Ha Kippah*."

I pulled out a British Survey map that I had recently purchased and unrolled it. Pesach moved closer, scrutinizing the chart.

"I can't find a name for this *wadi*," I stated.

Pesach puffed thoughtfully on his pipe, "You are right. It has no name. It's only about 800 meters long."

"Well," I remarked, "on this map we have a *wadi* without a name, and on the Copper Scroll we have a name (*Nahal Ha Kippah*) without a *wadi*."

Part Two

Digging Up the Future

Digging Up
the Future

*"Raising money for excavation is quite an
unpleasant chore. It means that one must
become a beggar, going to representatives of
endowments and organizations, trying to persuade
persons of wealth that the project in question
is both worthy and exciting."*
- The Archaeology of Palestine by W.F. Albright

I was on my own in the Valley of Achor. Pesach was busy with another archaeological dig at Beit Yerach and other sites. But he was able to consult with me while offering suggestions and encouragement. More than anything he was a wonderful mentor.

I returned to the Dead Sea caves several times and began to scout the area with survey maps in one hand and the translation of the Copper Scroll in the other. For several weeks I literally wandered around the Valley of Achor confining my search to an area, as described in Column 5, Line 13, of the Scroll, as a region *"on the way from Jericho to Succacah."*[1]

One day, my curiosity took me down a single dirt road that led from Ein Feshkah, the old resort of King Hussein. Walking south, I found myself staring up at a cliff line topped by a large dome-shaped formation. A mound or dome could be the *"kippah"* mentioned in the Copper Scroll. On September

18th of 1968, I found a massive cliff with a distinctive feature oriented toward the east. It was two large caves separated by a gigantic column. Directly behind the cliff, running north and south was a dry river bed. This was the same 800 meter wadi that had remained unidentified on all the surveys. Literally over-shadowing the entire site was the tallest line of cliffs, topped by that dome-shaped formation.

I had located:

o A twin cave with a massive pillar.

o The formation was adjacent to a wadi or dry nahal.

o A site overlooked by a dome.

o The area was "on the way from Jericho to Succacah."

This had to be the Cave of the Column by the River of the Dome as described in the Copper Scroll on Column 5, lines 12-13 also, Column 6 lines 1-3:

[5:12]   In the tomb which is in the River of the Dome

[5:13]   in the coming [way] from Jericho to Succacah, like this...

[6:1]   [beside the ?] Cave of the Column with two openings

[6:2]   entrances viewing East

[6:3]   in the North opening viewing Eastward

On that same day I ventured up onto the top of the twin caves and found a large hole in the roof. But it would be nine years before I began to dig at this site for the treasures of the Copper Scroll. In that time, I sifted the words of the Scroll, attempting to correlate sites referenced in the text. Eventually, Pesach and I would locate thirty such sites. Some were geologic in nature while others were geographic. They accurately matched corresponding terrain stretching from *Even Bohan* to the Canal of *Succacah.*

In 1977, we began our first excavation at the Cave of the Column. I was going to need a permit from the Israel Antiquities Authority. But I wasn't sure how to secure it. As I discussed this with Pesach, I had mentioned in passing that I had dug with Solly Steckoll. He scowled that he had written a very negative article on Steckoll and believed any scorn directed at Steckoll was deserved.

Before I could defend Steckoll, Pesach's eyes lit up when he realized that I had dug with Steckholl in June of 1967, under a permit from the Jordanian crown. There is a "grandfather clause" in Israeli law that would allow us to secure a permit based on my active participation on an authorized dig prior to the Israeli possession of Qumran, which occurred three months later in June of 1967. We got our permit and Pesach signed on as our required Israeli archaeologist.

Before we began that first dig, I rehearsed the Copper Scroll's text, knowing that we could depend on the physical features to guide us on our initial search. It was all there on the very first Column of the Scroll:

[1:5]   Here is the Miskhan (Tabernacle) on the third level, and the pieces of

[1:6]   gold (squiggle mark) In the large hole that is in the court (or large chamber) of the

[1:7]   pillar (column), deep in the wall that is covered [the] blue (which is)

[1:8]   opposite to the very high opening

[1:9]   in the tel (mound) [that is] blue

Compared to later digs, our first excavation at the Cave of the Column was a pretty modest beginning. It did not cost as much or require many workers. It only lasted thirty days and our expenses ran about three thousand dollars. Thanks to Larry and Louise Henneman, we were able to fund that excavation. We had some of our team in place, but needed more. So we took to the streets of Jerusalem. My son, Gershom, actually went up to total strangers and accosted them. We eventually rounded up enough to put about twenty volunteers to work.

Our first effort was in the upper chamber that I had discovered years ago. I climbed into it and showed Pesach the large hole and the corresponding line of text in the Copper Scroll. Pesach carefully reviewed the wording and scanned for physical characteristics of the chamber. If this was the hole mentioned in the Scroll, then there should be a hidden opening opposite the hole. There were numerous sizable stones on the floor of the chamber. One of these caught Pesach's eye. It was not large, but only the upper end was exposed.

My mentor and teacher Pesach Bar-Adon introduces me to the mysteries of the Judean Wilderness. Photo credit: Marvin Ellis

Pesach tapped the stone, "This stone is not natural here. Dig around it."

When it was exposed, it proved to be piece of solid granite which had been worn smooth by water. The stone was about 130 cm. long by about 90 cm. wide. It was approximately 30 cm. thick and weighed several hundred pounds. We managed to roll the stone over and discovered a hidden passage which led into the column side of the chamber, then angled northward into another larger cave in the rear. The descent continued for some 8 meters and bottomed out into a small, circular chamber that was 2.5 meters wide by 3 meters in length.

There was a red clay mound that was not natural to the site. It blocked the way, but we managed to climb over it. After a space of 6 meters, we found fill that almost reached the ceiling. I had fully expected to find the "blue" item referenced in the 7th line on the first Column of the Scroll.

I looked at Pesach and asked, "Where is the blue thing that is supposed to be here?"

He shrugged his shoulders, "*Nu* (So)?"

It would be eleven more years before I was to get my answer.

That dig did yield some curious artifacts that spoke to us through the centuries. As we dug our way through the first layer, we encountered thirty to fifty centimeters of sheep and goat dung indicating that Bedouins had recently used the cave as a sheepfold. There were also several tin containers near a fireplace on the northeast wall of the cave, and a sandal of the type worn by Bedouins.

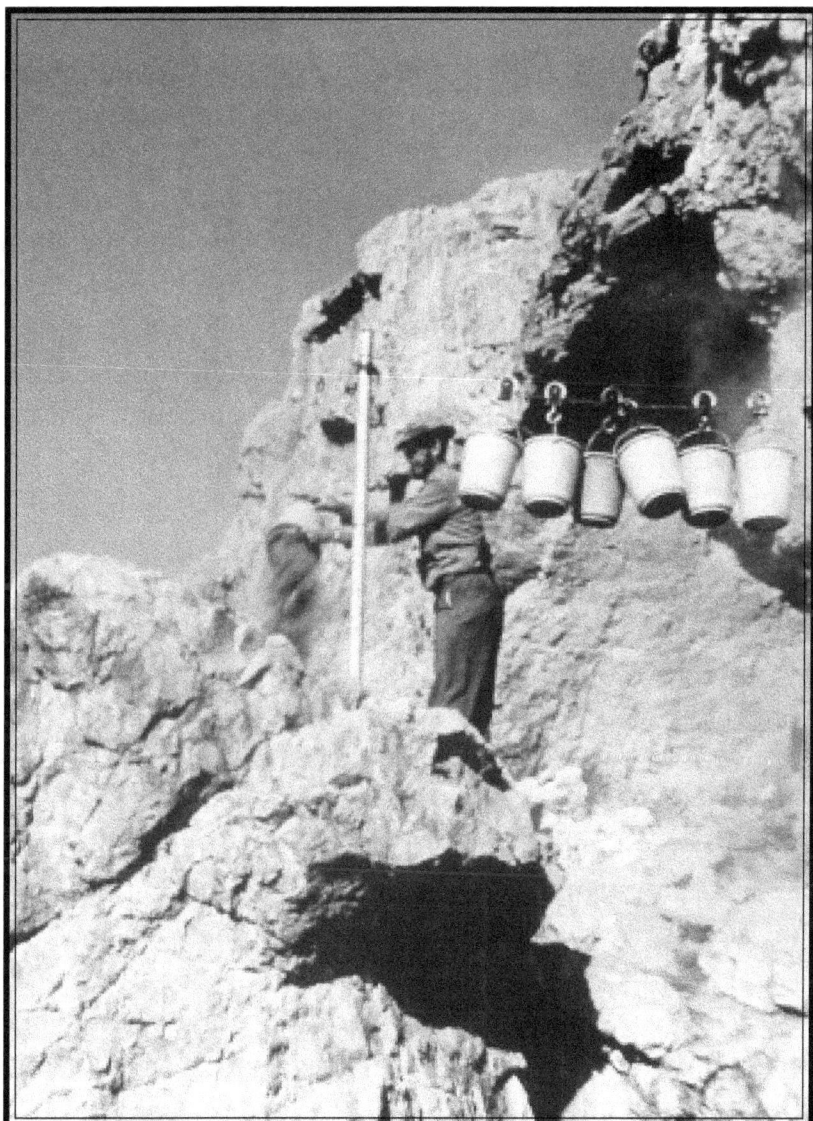

The 1977 dig season at the Cave of the Column was a modest affair in terms of the size of our team and our budget. That would change with subsequent digs. Photo credit:Anita Kiekhaefer

Forty centimeters under this level we found several spent rounds from an Enfield rifle and a broken china teacup, suggesting that British soldiers had occupied the cave before the Bedouin. The next layer in the stratum began approximately one meter below this surface, where we discovered levels of earlier Arab occupation. Beneath this was a Byzantine level of occupation with an abundance of Byzantine pottery shards. Under the Byzantine level were assorted stones of dolomite, weighing several hundred pounds each, along with pottery belonging to the late Roman period.

When the area was completely cleaned, we found that these large stones were laid on some kind of cement floor that had been poured from wall to wall. When we penetrated the cement floor we found yet another floor that resembled plaster. It ran throughout the entire cave. This floor was approximately 1.5 meters beneath the concrete floor and extended some 13-15 meters beyond the present opening of the cave. On the plaster floor there was a basket of peanuts, perfectly intact, except that the nuts had long since disintegrated within the shells.

We also unearthed shards of thin eating vessels, like those found by DeVaux in his excavation of the Qumran village. Under the plaster floor, there was a well-stratified presence of early Israelite occupation. On the bedrock beneath was an abundance of Calcolithic pottery with an altar containing the charred bones of sacrifices. Pesach couldn't have been more pleased. The site was unique and well stratified; to his knowledge there were no other sites of this type in Israel. Pesach was excited about the abundance of pottery found on each level. He collected the pottery in buckets which were then labeled with their respective occupation level.

Then one day, a group of scholars with École Biblique in Jerusalem arrived in long black Mercedes limousines. Pesach was nervous with excitement as he showed them the concrete and plaster floors along with the stratification of pottery that we had found on each level.

One of the École Biblique professors said, "It's really nothing.... it's nothing at all... we find these structures in all these caves... this is not plaster and this is not cement... it is entirely natural."

Pesach was crushed by their evaluation.

When they left he said, "I must take this data out of the report."

I told him that his notes about the floors were important and they must remain in the report, but Pesach would not relent. He removed each and every reference to the floors from his field notes. I told Pesach I would have the material analyzed. He agreed that it would be a good idea, but he added that even if we found it to be man-made, we still could not put it in the report after these "authorities" had designated it as simply natural.

I reminded Pesach that their unscientific imprimatur had already been used to seal the Qumran community as a group of celibate priests. De Vaux and company had made sure no one forgot that — by holding their daily Mass on the site. It didn't matter that Solomon Steckoll had produced evidence to the contrary with his excavations in 1967 and 1968, putting the whole monk story where it belonged — back in the dirt.

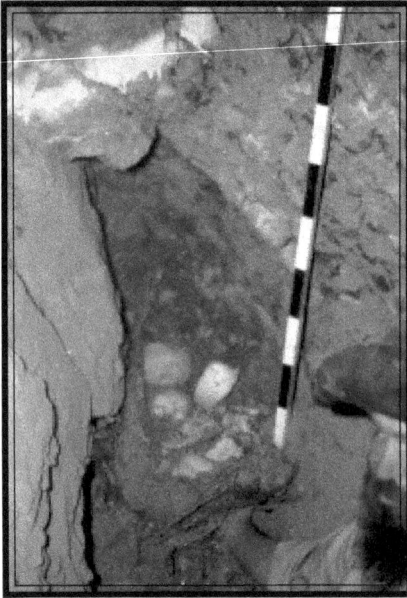

Remains of a Sumerian burial unearthed in the Cave of the Column.

I learned a valuable lesson on this first dig. I would not fall prey to opinion. I knew that geology would ultimately trump the opinions of a few so-called authorities.

Geology is the anatomy of the earth's body. The mountains and valleys are the wrinkles on the face of mother earth. In Hebrew, the word for a "spring" is *ein* or the "eye" where the earth is weeping. These springs and the rivers that flow from them form a habitat for all living creatures. Men build cities beside sources of water. It is therefore easy to see that geology and geography dictate the places where cultures flourish. They form the root of man's history.

Archaeology is the study of this history — turning over one page of earth at a time, reading in reverse, man's present to his past. Despite what the Discovery Channel may lead you to believe, archaeology is not a science and thus susceptible to opinion. Rather, archaeology is a discipline employing techniques borrowed from numerous sciences.

As new scientific technologies in geology and soil morphology emerge, so grows the number of sister disciplines which can be applied to deciphering, ever more accurately, the grammar that is written in the dust. Geological data can, for example, be used to make and/or confirm historical determinations as to age and climatic conditions that would otherwise be impossible. The collection of geological data should, therefore, precede all archaeological investigations.

The first archaeologist to make geology an issue was Dame Kathleen Kenyon. It was Kenyon who insisted that the composite layers of soil covering various levels of occupation should not be referred to as dirt or debris until after they had been thoroughly examined using soil morphology techniques. She said that only after it was removed from the site could it be referred to as simply debris.

After our experience during the 1977 dig, I was determined that we would not allow opinions to dictate our results. We were joined on later digs with an impressive line up of talent from the scientific ranks.

Larry Banks is a Senior Archaeologist for the US Army Corps of Engineers and has a degree in geology. As a geologist, he was the first to create and standardize a specific, scientific methodology for analyzing the layers of soil at an excavation site. He also performs a pollen dating calculation that can be used to determine the actual age of each level of occupation.

Banks has found that the sample stratum within the core drill contains a cyclical pattern of pollen data that accurately reflects seasonal and climatic changes throughout the year. The amount of pollen in any given year can be used to determine such things as whether crops were plentiful, or whether there was drought.

Others use epoxy spray to obtain samples. The exposed vertical surface of a cut is sprayed with a thick epoxy resin which penetrates the soil. When the epoxy dries, it can be pulled away to preserve a more accurate model of the stratum. This is a considerable improvement over gum tape. Of the three methods, the core drill sample remains superior, because it increases the accuracy of the analysis. It is important to emphasize, that while all of the techniques belong to the science of geology, they are now being applied to the discipline of archaeology. Our excavations at the Cave of the Column incorporated these techniques.

Notes

[1] Sometimes rendered as *Secacah*, one of the cities near the Dead Sea as found in Joshua15:60

Let's Do Lunch

*"Strip away the phony tinsel of Hollywood and you
will find real tinsel underneath."*
- Oscar Levant

In 1981, I was back home in Tyler, Texas, when I got a
phone call from one of my supporters.

"Vendyl, they've made a movie about you," he said.

"Who made a movie about me?" I asked.

"Spielberg — the guy that did 'Jaws' — he's made a
movie about your search for the Ark of the Covenant," he
replied.

Raiders of the Lost Ark, directed by Steven Spielberg,
was amazing filmmaking and a rip-roaring good time to be
had in the movie theater. At this point I should mention that
if someone in the legal department at Lucas Films is reading
this, you can put the phone down. I cannot help that my name
is Jones and that I happen to be looking for, among other
things, the Ark. I mention this because, in the past, well-
meaning friends and supporters have written letters and
made phone calls to the producers of *Raiders,* suggesting some
kind of promotional effort that would raise badly-needed
funds for an upcoming dig. They quickly learned that
Hollywood is populated with gatekeepers. Often these
supporters were met with curt denials that I even existed, or

were threatened with legal action for even having the audacity to suggest that there was any resemblance to persons living or dead.

Admittedly, I have enjoyed the notoriety that the film created, and have good-naturedly celebrated the parallels. More than once, I have walked to the podium at the start of a lecture and was greeted by someone playing a cassette or CD with John Williams' rousing march from the movie soundtrack. However, I want to make it clear, once and for all, that I have never stood up and declared, "I am the real Indiana Jones."

But the myth is so strong that, in one memorable instance, I told a newspaper reporter in Oklahoma City that I have never claimed to be the real you-know-who, yet in the following day's edition of the paper was a story that read, "The man who claims to be the Real Indiana Jones...."

Was the film based on me?

Proving that would take even better digging skills than I have. There are two tales about the development of the film. Possibly they intersect. I will attempt to provide you with the facts, without prejudice, as I have been able to discover them. You decide.

A San Francisco-based film maker by the name of Phil Kaufman read a book entitled The *Spear of Destiny* by Trevor Ravenscroft. The book is an almost hallucinatory account of Hitler's fascination with the occult — especially the 'Spear of Longinus' which allegedly pierced the side of Jesus, thus imbuing it with mystical powers. Hitler believed that possessing the spear would give him the power to rule the world. Ravenscroft also relates that Hitler had dispatched teams to acquire other holy relics. The Ark of the Covenant is mentioned, but only in a short paragraph. The book inspired Phil Kaufman to craft a screenplay.

About that time, George Lucas and Steven Spielberg were vacationing together in Hawaii, and they discussed collaborating on the film. They wanted to make an old-fashioned cliffhanger, like the serials shown during childhood Saturday matinees. Somehow they got wind of Kaufman's script. They bought it and agreed to give Kaufman a "story by" credit. Lawrence Kasdan was hired to re-write the scenario to fit the Spielberg/Lucas vision of the film. Lucas maintains that the hero's name was always going to be Jones, and the nickname, "Indiana," came from his dog. He has gotten a lot of mileage out of that dog — I understand that the same animal was also the inspiration for the Wookie in *Star Wars*.

In film jargon, let us flashback to our first dig in 1977. A writer by the name of Randy Fillmore joined our crew, almost by accident. He had come to Israel hoping to do a profile on the Israeli army. The IDF wouldn't allow the young writer any access. Fillmore went looking elsewhere for a story and hoped that he might find it on a *kibbutz*. Then he met some of the volunteers on our dig. Smelling a good story he joined the team. We spent hours together talking about the work. He wrote everything down, even taking notes when I would teach from the Bible in the evening.

The more Randy learned, the more intrigued he became by the story possibilities that the Copper Scroll offered, with its references to the Tabernacle and its riches.

It may be hard to believe now, but I was not thrilled that Randy would work the Ark into the plot.

I told Randy, "No one cares that I am looking for a two-thousand-year old pot of ashes. In fact, they think I am out of my mind. But if you write that we are also searching for the Ark, every jackleg will be over here in our way looking for it."

I cannot recall if he wrote a screenplay or a manuscript for a novel. The last time that I heard from Randy Fillmore, he had secured representation with a literary agent in New York. After that, the agent disappeared with Randy's material and that was the last he heard of anything resembling his story until he saw *Raiders of the Lost Ark* at his neighborhood theater.

Did Fillmore's script make its way to the West Coast and into the hands of a producer who showed it to Kaufman? Did it cross the desk of Spielberg or Lucas? I really don't care.

There are a couple of additional notes about the film. The female lead, played by Karen Allen, is called Marion Ravenwood, possibly a nod to the author, Trevor Ravenscroft. The other item that I find particularly fascinating is that the climax of the movie, as conceived by Lawrence Kasdan, was originally a chase sequence involving runaway mining cars. Those scenes run for several pages in the original screenplay, while the opening of the Ark only takes up a page or two at the most.

Spielberg's Jewish roots kicked in and he removed the mine car sequence (using it in the sequel.) He then turned the opening of the Ark sequence into an unforgettable cinematic experience. It was more than just great story-telling; that sequence burned the image of the ark of God into the public consciousness. Prior to *Raiders* you could have asked ten people on the street to describe the Ark, and all ten would have told you about a boat.

A network television crew visits the site during the 1998 dig in front of the Spice Cave.

For that, I am thankful, because our support base grew following the success of the film, and the press came calling. I was treated to several lunches with Hollywood types who wanted to put my story on the screen. Nothing ever came of those meetings. I have certainly put in considerable time in front of television cameras.

On one occasion, a Japanese television crew asked if we could film a segment with one of their rock stars at the cave site. It was funny watching us stumble over the rocks, me in my khakis and the long-haired singer in his black leather pants. We chatted nonchalantly like the best of friends each in our native tongue, as if we understood each other perfectly.

Even with the inevitable comparisons and questions regarding me and the screen Jones, I appreciate more than anything how the movie actually brought people to Torah. Some may laugh at such a statement — but great waves start as a small ripple.

We would witness the immediate fallout from the film by the time we began our next dig in 1982. We had to literally turn volunteers away.

Making Dust

Digging in Israel during the winter might be a little more inhospitable than you would imagine — unless you're digging near the Dead Sea. That is one of the wonders of Israel; its collection of macro climates all crowded within a few miles of each other. Our team of eager volunteers discovered that when we began digging in the Cave of the Column during February of 1982. The team began excavating these massive chambers that are located on the North face of the cliff, but the giant twin portals are actually oriented toward the East. Again, this is a feature referenced in the Copper Scroll.

Our ranks had swollen to over sixty volunteers. The volume of dirt in the massive chambers required all of us digging full time to empty the debris from the caves. The threat of walls collapsing was constant, but we remained injury free. We were successful in getting to bedrock and on the way unearthed some interesting artifacts. In facat, just three days into the dig, we found pieces of pottery from the Roman period. Near the surface we found a peculiar ring formation of seven rocks — with one in the center. When the center rock was removed, the remaining rocks around it were pulled upright, remaining in a circular pattern.

During that dig, I kept my promise to Pesach that I would not fall prey to opinion. A professional by the name of Dick McGlathery of Oklahoma City joined us that March. It was his geological appraisal that confirmed that the floors we had encountered some years before were cultural or man-made. It was also on this dig that we did a complete survey and mapping of the caves, led by Johnny Powell and Carl Clayton. They were assisted by Irv Hall, Bettye Heathcock, Shirley Roberts and Destry Blanchett.

Another highlight of the dig was the visit by the late Rabbi Sholomo Goren, of Blessed Memory. It meant so much to me that this great and holy man of G-d blessed us with his presence. In 1948, at the age of thirty, he became the first Chief Rabbi for the Israeli Defense Forces. My friend, Mati Pelet (who has also passed away), told me a wonderful story about Rabbi Goren. It was during the Sinai Campaign in 1956 — and Mati was leading a dangerous 15 day operation. Late one Friday afternoon, Rabbi Goren halted the operation to set camp for Shabbat. Mati argued that they were in a desert and did not have enough water.

Rabbi Goren told the colonel, "You are quoting Torah to me? That is what our ancestors also told Moses. But they still observed Shabbat! If we guard the Shabbat, G-d can give us water from the rock."

The rabbi outranked Mati, so they observed Shabbat. Only a few days later, the unit came upon a spring called Ein-Fortiga. The men refilled their canteens while Rabbi Goren made a blessing and read from the Torah where Moses brought forth water from the rock.

In 1967, as the Israelis repelled the onslaught of Arab armies from the Promised Land, Rabbi Goren mounted a tank as it circled Jericho seven times on June 7th. He blew the *shofar* (ram's horn) as Joshua had done thousands of years ago at Jericho. Later that same day, he stood before the *Kotel* (Western Wall) cradling a Torah scroll in one arm and blowing the *shofar* with his other hand. I was making my way through Jerusalem at that very moment. It was my good fortune and maybe my destiny to be there.

When Rabbi Goren first visited our dig in 1982, it was not our first meeting. I was ready for his unyielding line of questioning. He grilled me about the *Kalal* and what could happen if we found it.

I told him, "First, all religious Jews would return to Israel."

"That's only partially correct," he responded, "when the *Kalal* is found ALL Jews will be religious. There won't be any Conservative, Reform or Traditional Jews because all will return as Observant Jews."

He quizzed me further on what our plan was when the *Kalal* was recovered. I turned to the volunteers and they all responded, "Don't touch it!"

Goren turned his gaze to the sixty or so dust-caked volunteers, "What church are you from?"

I told the rabbi that they were all from a variety of
religious backgrounds. He turned to me saying, "You have
come to Israel looking for a treasure. You have already found
a treasure. All of these people are truly a treasure. I cannot
believe this. I think *Mashiach* has come!"

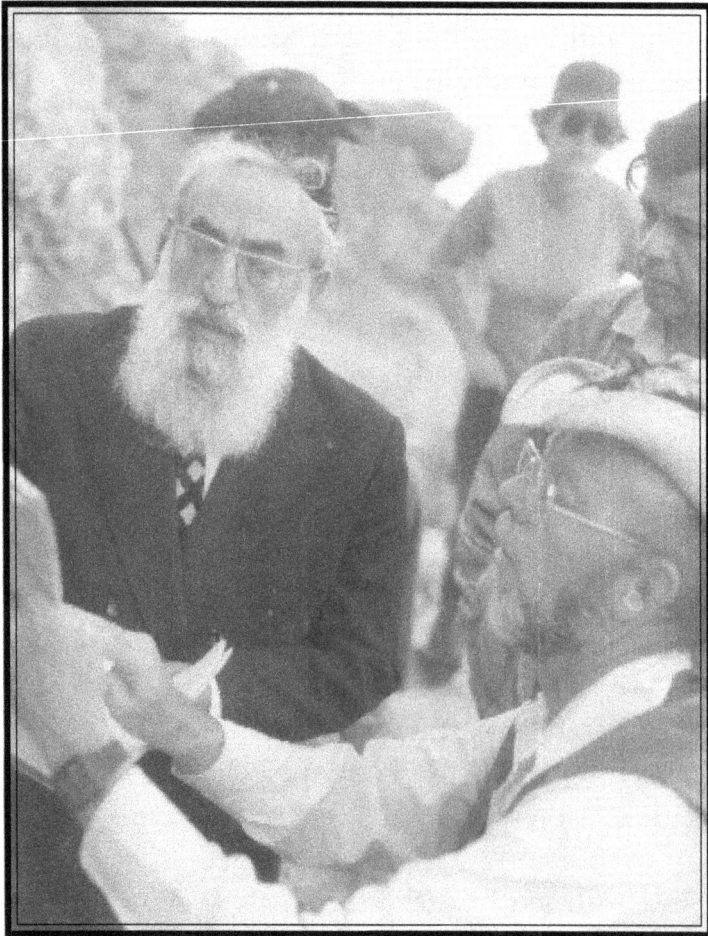

*The late Rabbi Shlomo Goren, of blessed memory, told the
volunteers, "You have already found a treasure. You are the
treasure!"*   Photo by Marvin Ellis

Rav Goren continued to be an active source of support and a fount of rabbinic wisdom. He made us aware of rare details in the Talmud and *Midrash*. One item in particular that he shared was that the lid of the *Kalal* fit inside the lip of the vessel's opening and that it was carefully sealed by the ring of the *Kohan Gadol* (High Priest). He also pointed out the reference to the *Parah Adumah* (Red Cow) in the *Siddur* (Hebrew Prayer Book) from a section called the Four Parshiot.[1]

During a break in the dig, I returned to Texas. That was when a chance meeting with Professor Mary Williams provided a valuable clue that would strengthen the link between the Copper Scroll and the Temple treasures. We had literally run into each other on the campus of the local university in Tyler. Professor Williams taught forensic handwriting; analysis employed in solving crimes such as check forgeries. She had heard of my work in Israel, but when she learned that I was using an ancient text from the Copper Scroll, she was intrigued and asked if she could examine it sometime. I was happy to oblige because it occurred to me that no one had ever thought to submit the Copper Scroll to that form of scrutiny. Her expertise might reveal some clues that others had missed. A few days later, I stopped by the office of Professor Williams with the hand-drawn transcription of the Scroll.

She thoughtfully scanned the letters. "This is just fascinating," she said, "and I don't know the language but I can already tell you that this was the work of **five different people**."

I was so taken aback that I didn't reply.

She continued to study the pages, "Something else that I can see here — the writers apparently grew tired and would allow another to take over; and sometimes they changed in the middle of a sentence. And look here, this one shows signs of strain, as if he were under duress."

I found her analysis to be both fascinating and unsettling. I had never considered that there was a team of people involved with authoring the Copper Scroll. The only thing I could do was to mentally file this surprising evidence away for future reference.

Notes
[1] See Chapter 2, "An Eternal Keepsake"
[2] Johnny W. Powell, PE, *Cave of the Column Survey Mapping*, Vendyl Jones Research Institutes, Arlington, Texas, 1995, p.86

Do You Speak Scroll?

Our 1982 dig had come and gone when I decided to re-marry.

Running back and forth to the Middle East to dig for months at a time, doing lectures across America, and begging for money to continue the digs, will exact a toll on a relationship — if both partners are not committed. I will spare you the details of my failed marriage, but will tell you that I do enjoy the matrimonial state and do not enjoy being lonely. Since my initial selection of a wife did not work out very well, I decided to let the task fall to someone who did it for a living. I sought out an Israeli matchmaker because, this time, I wanted a wife who would believe in the work, love Israel and who spoke Hebrew. I contacted Musa Khafri and gave him my wish list.

He introduced me to Zahava Cohen, a Haifa resident of Moroccan descent. I wasn't sure if I met her requirements for the ideal husband, but she more than met my expectations. She was fluent in Hebrew and Aramaic. Though she was a secular Israeli, she was a very learned one well-versed in Torah and Talmud. During our first meetings, when I explained to her the nature of my work, she was completely familiar with the historical and religious significance of the *Mishkan* and even the Ashes of the Red Cow. The fact that I had met someone who could trace their lineage to the *kohanim* had a special relevance.

We had what could be a described as a whirlwind courtship. Zahava was a widow with two growing boys, Yosi and Gadi. The older, Yossi, became part of our dig team, sometimes serving as photographer. He continues to work today in television production. Gadi went into business for himself, running a kosher food store in Dallas, Texas.

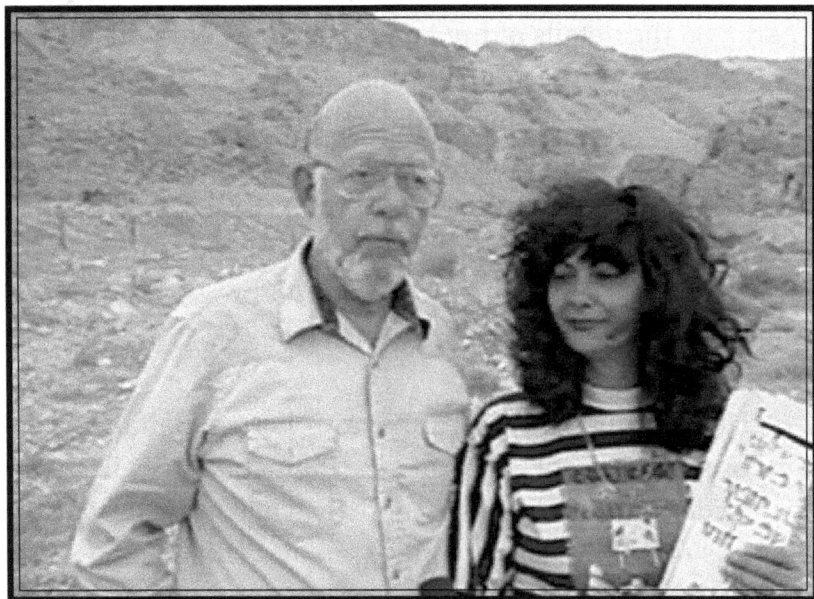

Zahava Cohen holding the transcription of the Copper Scroll text. Her understanding of the scroll led her to believe that a north cave would be worth investigating.

Since the beginning, I had depended on the transcriptions of John Allegro and Josef Milik. With all due respect, I found each of their versions lacking. Human nature being what it is, each interpreter brings his own prejudices to the task, sometimes their own shortcomings. The Copper Scroll, more than any Dead Sea Scroll, seems to evoke this response. Pick up five published versions of the Copper Scroll's text and you will get five diverse translations. My new bride proved to be a wonderful collaborator, especially in regards to my efforts to produce a translation that reflected the Mishnaic character of the Scroll.

Zahava understood rabbinical language. She also found and cataloged eighty-two non-words that had somehow made their way into the hand-drawn transcriptions. We visited Bruce Zuckerman's West Semitic Research in California. Zuckerman shot stunning, high resolution photographs of all 23 segments of the Scroll. Though he does not recommend using his photos to decipher the text, the clarity and detail in his photos make for a wonderful record, considering how badly the Scroll segments have deteriorated these past few years.

During our visit, Zahava showed him the list. Zuckerman explained that he and his associate, Al Wolters, had found roughly the same number of questionable words. These errors were published by Allegro and Milik. The mistakes might be attributed to the assistants who actually carried out the laborious task of duplicating the original words as they appear on the Scroll.

The next dig season, 1983, saw us return to the Cave of the Column — not only to excavate, but to map various chambers.

As Johnny Powell noted in his report, "the 1983 excavation survey took a radically new turn with the involvement of Colonel Mati Pelet."[2]

Mati Pelet was a former IDF Intelligence officer whose specialty was mapping.

Thanks to Mati, we were introduced to other experts in the field such as Professors Benyamin Schmutter and Yerachmiel Doucher from Technion Institute of Technology and Haifa University.

That same year, we uncovered remains of what Pesach determined was a Sumerian burial. Bar-Adon pointed out the use of a basket-like material and identified the find as Sumerian. In addition, the absence of pottery was another attribute of this period. When the find was submitted to the Department of Antiquities they classified it as Chalcolithic.

In the next few years we moved tons of dirt but not until 1988 would our dust, sweat and tears finally pay off.

The Golden Ark Explorer

During April of 1974, Bob and Margaret Lindsey graciously allowed me to stay with them and while browsing through their library I encountered a hefty 748 page tome, first published in 1931, entitled *Palestine Speaks*. It offered a wealth of historical facts, maps, charts, and photos from Biblical sites in the Middle East. I found concepts espoused by its colorful author that corresponded with my own search for treasures from the era known as the First Commonwealth of Israel.

The writer was a vigorous, self-styled adventurer who called himself the Pioneer Golden Ark Explorer. He tramped all around the Levant, driving the first automobile "to reach the Mount Nebo heights" — and posed for a pile of pictures. He also packaged tours to the Holy Land. Apparently, that endeavor wasn't enough to keep him busy, because he spent a good amount of time and energy searching for the Ark of the Covenant. He was A.F. Futterer and he believed that no guide worth his salt should undertake such an venture unless he knew first-hand what his clientele would experience.

"I touched, tasted, handled, ate, slept, walked, rode, suffered dangers and privations from the center of Arabia to Mars Hill in Athens. This is more than hearsay, it has come through the college of hard knocks to pave the way for your benefit. It is

*not like the man who wrote a book on 'How to Fly' who never
left the earth, and narrowly escaped death later in his first
practical ride in an aeroplane"*[1]

The old gentleman cut somewhat of a dashing figure.
Almost every photo in his book shows a sturdy, erect figure
striding along with a walking stick; his face framed by a thick
but neatly trimmed moustache and goatee. He resembled
"Colonel Sanders" in a pith helmet and leather puttees.

Palestine Speaks is part travel guide, part history book —
but mostly it is an arena for Futterer to espouse his religious
beliefs. He was equally unabashed in his support of the Jewish
people and made it crystal clear that the swelling Jewish
immigration rolls that he witnessed in Palestine, after World
War I, were a dramatic fulfillment of Biblical prophecies.

The old Ark explorer goes to great lengths in his book to
insure that the reader understands the import of the finding
the Ark. Here, he paraphrases Hillel the Great, from the
Second Temple era as the great sage describes the Torah kept
in the Ark:

> *"It contains the fundamental articles of our nation's
> constitution. It is the charter from God for a Nation's
> establishment and independence. It is a declaration of
> principles, which borne before us like a banner,
> proclaiming to the world for what we were to fight, for
> what we were to die. It is our confession of faith which
> we upheld before the world as Sacred, True and vital to
> the best interests of humanity..."*[2]

Futterer based his quest for the Ark on II Maccabees 2:1-6. When I read his thoughts on the treasures hidden by Jeremiah, I felt a measure of reassurance that someone who had trodden those desert paths before me had the same questions about those tantalizing words in the Book of Maccabees. Futterer was also convinced that there was so much more to be found along with the Ark.

"There must have been other Holy Vessels such as the Golden Candlestick, the Golden Table of Shewbread, the Tabernacle and many valuable rich robes and crowns. Jeremiah, a Levite, would be careful to leave nothing of sacred worth behind to be destroyed or stolen by the Gentile-Babylonians..."[3]

I never met the old gentleman but did meet an old business associate. It was while I was in Israel working with the Ministry of Defense on the Horst Empire project. Knocking off work one day, I decided to walk home instead of taking the bus.

Along the way, an old Arab man called to me in Hebrew, *"Slichah* (pardon), I hope you don't mind my asking, are you the one who is looking for the Ashes of the Red Cow?"

I had to pause briefly, wondering if someone had stuck a sign on my back, "Well, yessir, I am."

He motioned to the building behind him, "Please, would you have time for *cahwah?"*

He seemed friendly enough, so I accepted his invitation to join him. He introduced himself as Fareed Imam. While he poured hot aromatic coffee into diminutive ceramic cups, I browsed the room. The walls were lined with the shelves burdened by impressively bound texts. On each side of the shelves were old sepia-toned pictures that hung crookedly. The photographs spanned the years, full of dour faces shaded from the sun by their *kafiyahs*. There was history here.

We made small talk, until he went to his bookshelf and withdrew a Koran. He opened the worn pages searching for a particular commentary.

Fareed read aloud to me, "...the nation who possesses the ashes — all nations will submit to that nation."

I found the reference quite startling. Even the descendants of Ishmael were taught to expect the return of the sacred objects from Sinai. Looking around the room I thought I recognized an old photograph of A.F. Futterer.

"Do you know that old man?" I asked.

"Indeed," responded Fareed proudly.

He went on to share that he operated a travel agency in Jerusalem called Educational Tours, and that he always took care of Futterer's land arrangements. Fareed asked me if I remembered the photos of the car in Futterer's book. I nodded, and Fareed told me that it was the his car.

As far I know, Mr. Futterer never successfully launched a dig for the Ark. But he steadfastly maintained that should it be found; that modern descendants from the priestly line of Levi should be involved in returning the Ark to Jerusalem.

Of course, the old Nebo Explorer and I literally took different paths — theologically as well as archaeologically. In the latter realm, he haunted the goat paths around the hills of Moab. I believe he might have changed course if he had been aware of the Talmud and Midrash. These sources revealed a very different tale regarding the hiding place of the Ark and *Mishkan*. Futterer had never heard that there was an eighteen mile passage beginning under the Temple Mount and exiting in the Dead Sea Valley.[4]

According to rabbinic tradition, this secret tunnel was known only to the *kohanim* and to the king. While this tunnel would be the salvation of the holy treasures, it would prove to be the undoing of the last king to sit on the throne in Jerusalem. The account of King Zedekiah's capture, at the hands of the Babylonians, as described in II Kings 25:4 is important to us because it supports the tradition of a vast tunnel that led to the Judean wilderness:

"And the City was broken-up and all the men of war fled by the way of the gate between the two walls, which is by the King's garden. [Now the Chaldees were surrounding the city round about.] And the king [Zedekiah] went [out] by the way of the plain [Aravah]. And the army of the Chaldees pursued after the king, and overtook him in the plains [Aravah] of Jericho...."

The passage states that there is a *gate between the two walls.* There have been endless commentaries to address this allegedly problematic text. Bible scholars sometimes have a penchant for finding the most complicated way to explain a simple statement in the Scriptures. If one, however, seeks the simplest explanation of the text, he will discover the most profound answers.

The late Dr. James Grey said, "A great Bible teacher is not one that can express simple truths in great words, but rather one who can express great truths in simple words."

The simplest explanation can be found in the available Biblical sources. The Babylonian army had surrounded Jerusalem and was breaking down the walls. The only escape route was through the eighteen mile-long cavern. **Therefore, a gate should be found between the two walls of the cavern.**

Allow me to set the stage for this ancient and tragic siege of Jerusalem, that sent a monarch scurrying down an underground labyrinth to elude capture. We have to look further back in time to see the events that set this Babylonian war machine in motion.

Eight-year-old Josiah, the last righteous king of Judea, took the throne in the year 3285. Jeremiah would begin to utter his prophetic warnings during the young king's reign. When he was twenty years of age, Josiah began sweeping religious reforms. At twenty-six, he ordered repairs made on the Temple. A rare Torah scroll, written by the very hand of Moses, was discovered hidden under the stones in the Temple

The Gate Between Two Walls. Intrepid travelers can enter the Quarry of Solomon near the Damascus Gate. Once inside, you veer to the left and drop down a hole — if the guard on duty will let you. It's actually off limits to the general public.

floor. When they inspected this precious document, instead of being rolled to the Book of Genesis, they found the scroll wound at the 36th verse in the 28th chapter of Deuteronomy:

"The Lord shall bring you, and your king which you shall set over you, to a nation which neither you nor your fathers have known; and there shall you serve other gods, of wood and stone."

Jeremiah saw this as an explicit sign that Jerusalem would fall in the future. He convinced King Josiah to remove the Ark from the Holy of Holies, and to hide it along with the Breastplate, the Vestments of the High Priest, the Rod, the Anointing Oil and pot of Manna.[5]

It was the year 3303 from Adam.

King Josiah would later ride into battle against Pharaoh Necho II of Egypt. He fell in battle at the age of thirty-nine. It was the year 3316. His son, Jehoahaz took the throne but only reigned for three months. Judea, caught in the constant tug of war between their neighbors to the north and south, became a vassal to Egypt. They deposed Jehoahaz and installed his brother, Jehoyakim on the throne. The nation's fate was sealed by kings who defied G-d's prophets. Even some of the kohanim led the people astray.

From the north, Nebuchadnezzar stormed across the land, extending his rule from Babylon to Judea. Now, Jehoyakim served a new master and paid him heavy tributes. The Exile began to unfold as Nebuchadnezzar punished the leadership in Jerusalem, plundering part of the city and taking captives.

At the age of twenty-one, Zedekiah, was placed on the throne by Nebuchadnezzar who made him swear on a Torah scroll that he would not rebel. Zedekiah eventually broke his oath and made an alliance with Egypt. The angry Babylonian king sent his armies to raze Jerusalem and its Holy Temple to the ground.

On the ninth day of the fourth month, in the year, 3338, King Zedekiah and a small company fled the city by way of the Gate Between Two Walls. The last king to sit on the throne in Jerusalem was betrayed by a deer. A detachment of Babylonian solidiers were hunting near the Dead Sea. They spotted a deer running into a cave and gave chase. The soldiers ran headlong into the fleeing Zedekiah exiting the cave.

The language of II Maccabees 2:2-6 is not as exact as extant Jewish sources, but does relate briefly that some time prior to the destruction of Jerusalem, Jeremiah had launched a secret, but massive effort to remove the sacred Temple vessels. *Emek Ha Melekh* is richer in detail. From this source we learn how Jeremiah's five colleagues, Shimur HaLevi, Zedekiyahu, Yizkiyahu, Haggai the Prophet and Zachariyah, the son of Iddu the Prophet, carried out this sacred secret mission — with three hundred priests along with Levites "without number."

They removed all the treasures of the Tabernacle from under Moriah, and carried them through eighteen miles of the natural tunnel to a site near the exit of the passage in the Valley of Achor. This ocurred in the year 3331, a full seven years before the Temple was destroyed.

I believe that all of these various accounts converge and focus on the location of the hidden sacred treasures. To sum up once more:

☐ There was an ancient underground passage running from Jerusalem to the Aravah of Jericho (Dead Sea Valley).

☐ The passage was known to the priests and the king.

☐ Jeremiah transports the Temple treasures into chambers under the Temple Mount.

☐ Jeremiah's companion, Shimur Ha Levi, records the entire episode complete with an inventory of the treasures.

☐ The inventory is inscribed on a Copper Scroll.

☐ The king escapes under the Temple Mount passing through a gate between two walls and travels along an 18 mile passage.

☐ The king emerges from that 18 mile passage in the Dead Sea Valley.

☐ Just over 2,600 years later, the Copper Scroll is found in a cave in the Dead Sea Valley.

☐ The Temple Scroll which also references the Copper Scroll is unearthed Cave 11, near the Copper Scroll cave.

☐ The Holy Anointing Oil is found in the vicinity of the Copper Scroll Cave.

The Holy Incense is also found in the same area.

Notes
[1] Futterer, Palestine Speaks, published by A.F. Futterer, Los Angeles, 1931, p.14
[2] ibid, p. 543
[3] ibid, p.549
[4] Rabbi Shlomo Rotenberg, Am Olam: History of the Eternal Nation, Keren Eliezer Pub., Brooklyn, NY, 1988, p. 157
[5] ibid, p.108

The Valley
of the King

The concept that the Copper Scroll listed treasures from *Beit Ha Mikdash* (Solomon's Temple) and therefore contained such fabled lost artifacts as the Ark of the Covenant, was validated thanks to the efforts of Rabbi Rachmael Steinberg and Rabbi Mendel Tropper. I am deeply indebted to them for undertaking the laborious task of finding those *other records* referenced in II Maccabees. They brought to my attention a remarkable source called *Emek HaMelekh*, a rare kabbalistic text published in Amsterdam in the year 1648. The text on the Marble Tablets (*Massaket Kelim*) matches that of *Emek HaMalekh*, except for the first paragraph. Inscribed at the beginning of the Marble Tablets we read:

> *"These are the words of Shimur HaLevi, the servant of HaShem. In the year 3331 of Adam."*

Of course, that event is the sealing away of the Tabernacle treasures for thousands of years.

The author was Rabbi Naftali Hertz Ben Ya'acov Elchanon. He was known as a master teacher, well-versed in the mystical aspects of the Oral and written Torah. To underscore his pedigree, we know that he came from a line of scholars that led back to another eminent Torah teacher and kabbalist, Rabbi Isaac Ben Solomon Luria. Known as the

Ari, he led a community of mystics at Safed, in Israel around 1538. The group included another Torah giant, Rabbi Yosef Caro, of Blessed Memory, who authored the *Shulchan Aruch*.

Rabbi Hertz cites his source from an almost forgotten addition, or *Tosefta*, to the Talmud, in Mishnah 3 under the section of Kelim[Vessels]. Some scholars have rightly charged that they fail to find any mention of a Copper Scroll, Marble Tablets, Ibex Scroll and Silver Scroll in the *Tosefta*. It is simply because those references are missing from modern copies of the *Tosefta*. As previously noted, with the exception of the reference to the year, *Emek HaMelekh* repeats the entire text of *Massaket Kelim*, inscribed on the Marble Tablets found in vaults of the museum in Beirut, Lebanon.[1]

These *mishnayot* or records carry an amazing inventory of fabled vessels that were fashioned in the very shadow of Mount Sinai over 3,000 years ago. Among these astonishing treasures are the Breastplate of the High Priest, the Table of Showbread, the Priestly Garments of Aaron, the Rod, the container of Manna, the Menorah and the fabled Ark of the Covenant along with the Tabernacle itself.

As I mentioned in the previous chapter, all of these sacred instruments were first removed from the Temple under the direction of King Josiah and the prophet Jeremiah. Years later, in 3331 the prophet would oversee an even more ambitious removal so that the sacred vessels would be completely out of harm's way when the Babylonians destroyed Jerusalem.[2]

Transporting these items from the temple to their hiding places was conducted under a veil of secrecy. This was easily accomplished, since the Temple Mount is honeycombed with caverns, many of them sealed unto this day. The operation was supervised by five *zadokim* (righteous men) whose names are found in *Masseket Kelim*. These remarkable heroes are Shimor Ha Levi, Zedekiah, Haggai the Prophet, Zechariah the Prophet, and Hezekiah. Keep in mind some of these amazing figures are the very same prophets whose books are found in your Bible.

When you read the following text keep in mind these very key points:

☐ This record states that the holy treasures of Solomon's Temple were hidden and the places of their concealment were written on **copper**.

☐ Handwriting analysis confirmed that there were **five authors** who wrote the text of the Copper Scroll.

☐ *Emek HaMelekh* states that there were **five authors**.

Here is the English translation of Rabbi Hertz's *Emeq HaMelekh* (Valley of the King)

These Mishnayot were written by five righteous men. They are: Shimor the Levite, Hizkiyahu, Zidkiyahu, Haggai the Prophet and Zechariah, son of Ido the Prophet. They concealed the vessels of the Temple and the wealth of the treasures that were in Jerusalem which will not be discovered until the day of the coming of Mashiach, son of David, speedily in our times, Amen, and so it will be.

Mishnah 1

These are the vessels dedicated and concealed when the Temple was destroyed: The Tabernacle and the Curtain, the Holy Menorah, the Ark of Testimony, the golden forehead Nameplate, the golden crown of Aharon the Cohen, the Breastplate of Judgment, the silver Trumpets, the Cherubim, and the Altar of burnt offerings, the Curtain of the Communion Tent, the forks and the bread molds, the Table [of the Showbread], the Curtain of the Gate, the Copper Altar, the sacred garments of Aharon which were worn by the Cohen HaGadol (High Priest) on the Day of Atonement, Pa'amonim (bells) and Rimonim (pomegranates) on the hem of the robe [of the Cohen Gadol], the holy vessels that Moses made on Mount Sinai by the command of the Holy One, the Staff, and the Jar of the Manna.

Mishnah 2

These are the holy vessels and the vessels of the Temple that were in Jerusalem and in every place. They were inscribed by Shimur HaLevi and his companions, on a "Luach Nehoshet" (Copper Plate), with all the Vessels of the Holy of Holies that Shlomo son of David made. And together with Shimur were Hizkiyahu, Zidkiyah, Haggai the Prophet, and Zechariah, son of Berachiah, son of Ido the Prophet.

The classic Emek Ha Melekh exhaustively details the sacred treasures and their hiding places. First written in 1648 by Rabbit Naftali Hertz, it was recently republished in Hebrew.

Mishnah 3

These are the Vessels that were taken by (buried in) the ground: the locking rods, the pegs, the boards, the rings, the standing pillars of the courtyard. These are the Vessels: 1,200,000 silver Mizrakot (sacrificial basins); 50,000 Mizrakot of fine gold; 600,000 (?) of fine gold, and 1,200,000 of silver. These five [men] *inscribed these Mishnayot in Babylon together with the other prophets that were with them, including Ezra the Cohen, the Scribe.*

Mishna 4
Of the Levites, 130 were killed and 100 escaped with Shimur HaLevi and his companions. These [men] concealed 500,000 trays of fine gold, and 1,200,000 of silver; 500,000 bread molds of fine gold, and 1,200,000 of silver. On each of the molds, there were 5 Margaliot (pearls?) and 2 precious gem stones. The value of each precious stone was 100 talents of gold, and the total value of all the Margaliot was 200,000 talents of gold. There were also 36 golden Trumpets. All of these were hidden and concealed in a tower in the land of Babylon, in the great city called Bagdat. [There was also a 7-branched] Menorah of fine gold, [worth] 100,000 [talents], with 7 lamps on each [branch], 26 precious gem stones on each Menorah, each Margalit (pearl? gem?) priceless, and between every gem stone, 200 [smaller] stones, also priceless.

Mishnah 5
There were 77 tables of gold, and gold [hangings] from the walls of the Garden of Eden that was revealed to Shlomo. Their radiance was like the brilliance of the sun and the moon that shine above the world. And all the silver and gold that ever existed in the world, from the six days of creation until the day that Zidkiyahu became king, did not equal the value of the gold that was overlaid on the Temple from within and from without. There is no end, no measure, no set amount, and no weighing

of the gold that overlaid the Temple and the face of the Temple. All this, plus another 7,000 talents of gold, were brought and concealed in the "Segel Habar" (?) with precious stones with which the Temple was built, besides 3 rows of priceless stones and one row of Almugim (coral?) trees. [Of] the three rows of priceless stones, the length of each row was 7 cubits, and width 5 cubits, [of the cubits] established by David. The length of one Margalit (pearl? gem? building stone?) was 10 cubits. David prepared all of these for the Great House (Temple), for Shlomo, his son.

Mishnah 6
The number of [building?] stones was 36,000, the same as the number of gem stones. From all these the Temple was built. There were also three-plus-one rows of Almugim trees, overlaid with fine gold and placed in the building. All those were hidden from Nebuchadnezzar by the fittest [men] of Israel. The Almugim shine like the brilliance of the firmament (sky).

Mishnah 7
The counting of precious stones, Margaliot gems, silver, and gold that King David dedicated to the Great Temple was: 1,000,000 talents of silver, 100,000 talents of gold and trees made of "Parvaim Gold" which bore fruit, 600,000 talents of fine gold from beneath the Tree of Life in the holy Garden. All these were revealed to Hilkiyah the Scribe, who gave them into the safekeeping of the angel Shimshiel to guard until King David arises, to whom he will hand over the silver and gold, including the gold that Shlomo contributed, and

*the talents of gold and priceless precious stones.
All these were concealed, hidden, and safeguarded
from the army of the Chaldeans in a place called
Borseef.*

Mishnah 8
*There were 7 golden Curtains that contained
12,000 talents of gold. There were 12,000 garments
of the Levites with their belts, and the Ephod (vest)
and Meil (robe) of the Cohen Gadol which he wore
when he performed the Temple service. In addition,
there were 70,000 garments worn by the Cohanim,
with their belts, their turbans, and their pants.
David made all of these for them to atone for Israel.
And the fittest [men] of Israel took them secretly, as
they had been instructed. All this service-gear was
[concealed] until the future to atone for Israel [in
the end of days].*

Mishnah 9
*David [also] made 1,000 lyres and 7,000 harps to
atone for Israel. He had Zilzalim (cymbals) for
singing, extolling, thanksgiving, and praising the
G-d of Israel which were handed down to him from
Moses, from Sinai. The words, "From beneath the
legs of the Throne of Glory, sapphire stone, in the
likeness of the Throne" (cf. Exodus 24:10), were
inscribed upon them. The lyres were made of
Almugim wood, overlaid with fine gold, with 8
stones on each lyre, carried by the clouds, the
demons and the spirits that were under Shlomo's
dominion. On each lyre was a bell of "Nehoshet
Kalal" (burnished copper) from before the Throne
of Glory, together with a priceless, precious stone*

that Moses quarried on Mount Sinai from under the Throne of Glory which was upon the Sapphire Stone. All these were hidden and concealed in "Ein Zidkiyah" that the fittest [men] of Israel knew in secret, lest they fall, G-d forbid, into the hands of the enemy who hated Israel. For these vessels are not to be used except to atone for Israel. Baruch [ben Neriah] and Zidkiyahu thus concealed them to prevent the Chaldeans from using them, G-d forbid. They hid them until the day when Israel will return to their former stature and reclaim [eternal] honor and wordly glory, and they find a man whose name is David, son of David. The silver and gold shall then be unearthed to him, when all Israel shall gather and make a complete Aliyah (ascent) to Jerusalem. Amen.

Mishnah 10

These are the weights of silver concealed at "Ein Kahal" by Baruch and Zidkiyah: 1,200,000 talents of silver, 1,600,000 of fine silver. Copper vessels: 2,000,000 pots of fine copper, and 1,100,000 of iron; [Countless] Shefatim (type of pot) without Metzukim (ladles) and copper Metzukim around the copper gate; countless Cherubim; countless copper sinks/lavers; 3,000 frying pans of fine gold; 70 priceless tables of fine gold from beneath the Tree of Life standing in the holy Garden, upon which were placed the Showbread. Golden Shekamim (type of tree) with all manner of delicacies hanging from them. They are all made of refined gold which David, King of Israel, refined. All those were concealed by Zidkiyah.

Mishnah 11

Treasures of gold and silver [stored away] from the days of David until Zidkiyah and until Israel was exiled to Babylon: Hundreds of thousands of golden shields, and countless silver [shields]; 1,353,000 precious stones and fine stones. All of these were hidden and concealed in the wall of Babylon and in Tel Bruk under the big willow tree in Babylon upon which they hung their lyres (cf. Psalm 137:2). And from the House of the Forest of Lebanon (i.e. the Temple), they took 1,900,000 Korin (measures) of gold. All the prophets, wise men, and scribes [in the world] could not calculate the wealth and the glory that was in Jerusalem.

Mishnah 12

Hiluk, son of Shimur HaLevi, was given twelve more precious stones in order to hide them so that they could [eventually] be restored to the Tribes [of Israel]. The names of the Tribes were engraved on them, and they shone on the Tribe's heads, excellent and precious, one more than the other. No king, prophet, or anyone else knew where they were hidden, excepting Hiluk, son of Shimur HaLevi. The remainder of the wealth and glory that was in Jerusalem was taken by angel Shimshiel. Shimur, Hiluk, and their companions, the Levites, later went and showed it to Michael and Gavriel. All Israel concealed the Vessels until a righteous king arises over Israel. What's more, they all swore a solemn vow never to reveal the whereabouts of these vessels until David, son of David, arises. All silver, gold, and Margaliot (precious stones) which was ever hidden away will be handed over to him when the exiles of Israel will be gathered from the four ends of the earth, and they ascend with greatness and exaltation to the land of Israel. At that time, a great river will issue forth from the Holy of Holies of the Temple. Its name is Gihon, and it will flow to the great and dreadful desert, and become mixed with the Euphrates River. Immediately, all the Vessels will float up and be revealed.

Notes

1 Al Wolters, "Apocalyptic and the Copper Scroll", *Journal of Near Eastern Studies*/Volume 49, January-October 1990, University of Chicago Press, p. 147

2 Babylonion Talmud, *Horayot* 12A

Oil of Gladness

Moses took the anointing oil, and anointed the Tabernacle and all that was in it, and sanctified them. And he sprinkled it upon the altar seven times, and anointed the altar and all its utensils, both the basin and its pedestal, to sanctify them. And he poured of the anointing oil upon Aaron's head, and anointed him, to sanctify him.
- Leviticus 8:10-12

The excavations at the Cave of the Column were becoming a full time job. By 1988, we were spending a minimum of forty five to sixty days digging. To handle the amount of dirt and debris that we were hauling out of the caves, we assembled some $200,000 dollars worth of conveyor equipment. The volunteers would come in shifts, some for a few weeks, others a month, possibly longer. Our excavations were broken into three main phases. The actual dig was book-ended by two weeks at the beginning and another two at the close of the excavation. We had a small seasoned gang who dealt with the basics like food, lodging, transportation, insurance and shaking dust off the mattresses.

Once things got under way the work was tedious and the hours are long. Hiking up the steep rocky slopes around the caves will quickly remind you that maybe that extra Twinkie was one too many. There are jagged piles of stones that chew into the sole of your shoes and fine soil that dusts

everything a pale brown. You also deal with 100 plus
temperatures when the dig season stretches into May and
June. By ten o'clock in the morning, the sun is baking the
arid cliffs and you think you've stepped into an oven. Oddly,
getting sunburned is a rarity. It has something to do with the
region being at the deepest place on the surface of the earth.

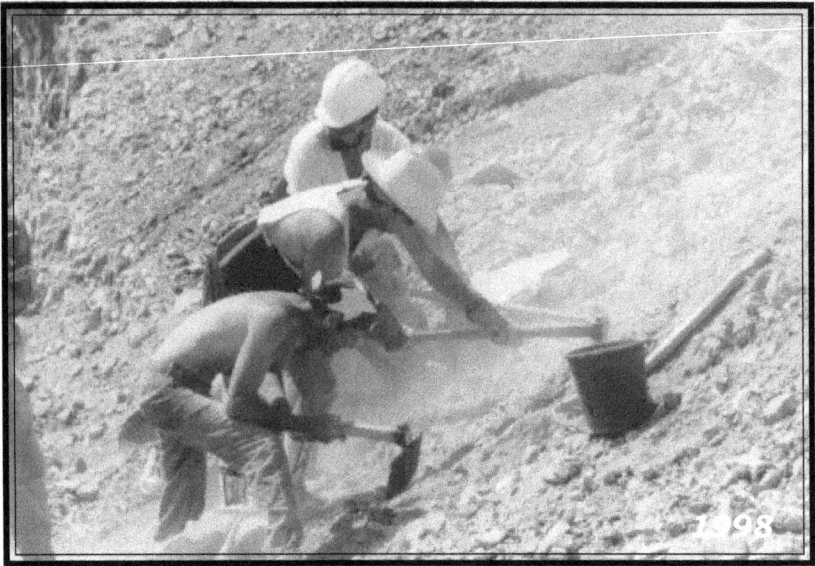

The flies at Qumran are a special breed. When you swat
them, they are just stunned. They drop, kick around for a
few seconds then fly away. The other varmints that make the
dig site interesting are a species of very large scorpions. The
black ones remind me of a variety that I have seen in Mexico.
But there is a scorpion that lurks in the Judean wastes that
will haunt your dreams – it is an almost iridescent green and
the size of your hand. Somehow we manage to ignore all of

these things and get down to the business of clearing a quadrant or a cave.

There are small pleasures to be experienced during long hours spent scraping soil and debris. Sunrise at Qumran is an unforgettable visual treat. The morning light coats the cliffs with a shimmering wash of gold from the Creator's finest palette. Later in the day, if you look up past the cliff line you will see a deep azure sky that matches the blue colors of the Israeli flag. Water tastes better than you ever remember, a breeze feels like a gift and you will feel the sweetest slumber that night.

In 1988, we began to spread the work to other caves in the vicinity of the Cave of the Column. My own Institute for Judaic-Christian Research carried on excavations in a joint effort with the Institute of Archaeology of Hebrew University in Jerusalem. Per our agreement with the IAA to have a recognized archaeologist on the permit, we hired Joseph (Yosi) Patrich who was assisted by Benny Arubas and Benny Augur.[1]

Start at the popular tourist site featuring the ruins of Qumran and follow the dirt road north, past Kibbutz Kalia, within a mile, there is the Cave of the Column looming on the left. Keep going for another half-mile and you will be in the general vicinity of a little cave where we made our first major discovery.

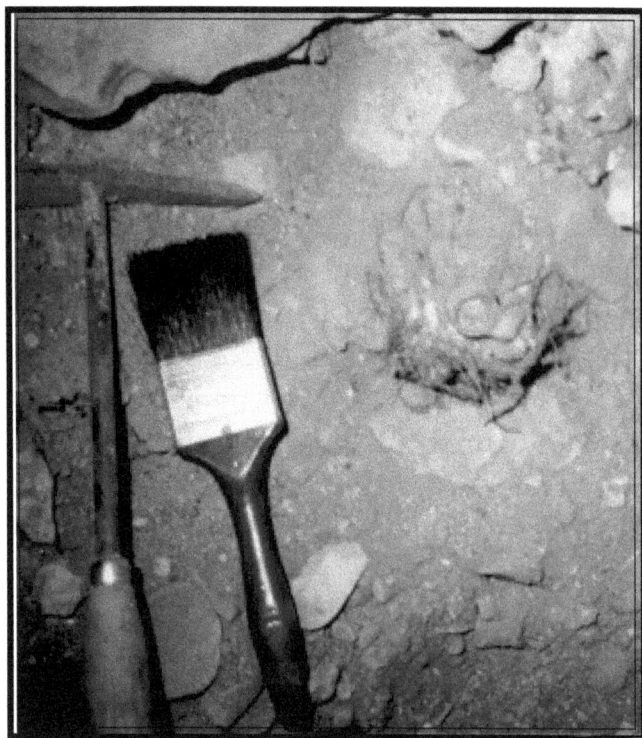

The clay juglet of oil 'in situ' as discovered in 1988.
Photo credit: Larry Johnson

When excavation first began, the diggers found mostly debris and pottery that revealed Roman occupation. Our team hit bedrock pretty quickly in the southern part of the cave near the entrance. The finds at this point were from three periods: the Chalcolithic, Iron Age II and Early Roman periods. On the northern end of the chamber we found two pits. In the narrow pit closest to the entrance, about three feet down we unearthed an object small in size but enormous in worth. It was a diminutive clay pitcher about five inches in height. The little vial held around three ounces of thick reddish oil. The find was still wrapped in date palm fibers to protect it. In the hours after its discovery, the juglet sat out in the one hundred degree heat and its contents, according to some gave off a sweet smell.

Our team had found a container that held an oil of unknown origin. The historian Pliny recorded that it was in this very region of ancient Israel where a substance called persimmon oil (*Shemen Afarshimon*) was manufactured. It was the product of a now extinct type of persimmon bush. The plants were grown along the shores of the Dead Sea near Ein Gedi and jealously guarded by Israel. The Romans took all of the little trees back to Italy but they died. Apparently they will only flourish below sea level. The oil was also called balsam. Segment 12, Line 2 of the Copper Scroll references hidden "juglets" while "oils" are mentioned in the same of column of the scroll on Line 12.

Was our discovery the aforementioned oil or juglet and di it contain the *Shemen Ha Mishchah*, also known as the *Shemen Afarshimon*?

Since the Torah forbids manufacturing anything like it, the original formula as compounded by Moses was the only one sanctioned for the anointing of the High Priests and the Kings of Israel. Like the sacred treasures from Solomon's

The clay vial containing Shemen Afarshimon *wrapped in date palm fiber. When left in the sun, a thick black syrupy substance began to leak from a crack in the juglet.*   Photo credit: Yossi Cohen

Temple, this Holy Anointing Oil was concealed before the fall of the First Temple as recorded in the Talmud.[2] After that time, the balsam oil was used for the purpose of anointing. This was the case when the prophet Elisha anointed Jehu in 1 Kings 19:16.[3]

During the entire four hundred twenty year period of the Second Temple, there were three hundred High Priests — **none** of whom were anointed with the original *Shemen Ha Mishchah*.

The word *Messiach* or Messiah (anointed one) is derived from *Shemen Ha Mishchah*. Exodus 25:6 and Exodus 30:24 detail the preparation of the oil. A small amount was used to anoint the Tabernacle, the Ark and the vessels of the Tabernacle. In addition, Aaron was anointed as High Priest. G-d, in the Torah, states that the anointing is, *"To Me..."* which means that the oil marked whatever it touched as *kadosh* (holy), dedicated for the Creator. Since a king of Israel is sanctioned by the Creator, the oil was used on King David who was anointed by the Prophet Samuel. Only kings descended from David could be anointed with this very same oil.[3]

The text might lead the reader to conclude that the oil was liberally poured over the head of the anointee. But the ritual was done by making the letter *kaf* (for kohen) on the forehead of the one being anointed. Even so, the oil might trickle down into the beard, as described in Psalms 133. A king was anointed by the oil being drawn around the forehead and scalp like a crown.[4]

A sample was extracted from the juglet and analyzed by Zeev Aizenshtat and Dorit Aschengrau at Hebrew University. By the time it had arrived at the lab any hint of fragrance had completely vanished. The sample was subjected to a series of tests which resulted in the following conclusions:

· The oil was from plants.
· It was not a resin.
· The oil was remarkably well preserved.
· It was not olive oil.[5]
· The consistency of the oil resembled balsam.

Everyone connected with the discovery, especially Professor Patrich felt strongly that this sample yielded a substance that was very likely the balsam oil. At least that's what he told the Associated Press in 1989.[6]

Exodus 30:22 lists the main ingredients for compounding this oil as myrrh, cinnamon, cane (possibly an extract from the calamus plant) and cassia all in **liquid** form. These elements were blended with water and allowed to soak. Later, olive oil was added and the mixture placed over heat until the water evaporated and the oil had completely absorbed the essences.[7]

At first glance it might appear that this exciting find was not *Shemen Afarshimon*. Some might rush to judgment, citing a missing essential ingredient — the olive oil. Not being as stable, the olive oil would have dissipated after 2,000 years, leaving only the hardier residues of other plant oils intact. It is important to note that the four oils listed in

Exodus 30:22 were only the **main ingredients**. The remaining essences came from the same spices as found in the *Qetoret*. This is significant because one of those spices was the rare balsam. I believe this particular ingredient in the *Shemen Afarshimon* was so resilient that its residue is what remained in the juglet long after its own fragrance had vanished.

After the results from the testing were announced, the news of the discovery spread worldwide. The Associated Press carried the story and the February 15, 1989 edition of the New York Times also trumpeted the find. In the weeks that followed we saw coverage from every major broadcasting network, including CNN. The following year, write-ups continued in such publications as the October '89 issue of National Geographic and the December installment of Omni Magazine.

The discovery of the oil also brought into sharp focus what Ben Zion Luria had written regarding the Copper Scroll:

"...the validity and authenticity of the Copper Scroll would remain in question until one single item mentioned in the scroll is discovered. Once something is found at Qumran that is listed among the 64 designated items and places, the scroll's validity will be unquestioned."[8]

The Copper Scroll lay entombed and ignored in the Museum of Amman, Jordan for over 20 years. Thanks to this little clay vial there was renewed interest in the scroll.

The larger issue for me was that this might be a clear-cut indication that we were on the right track. If Luria was correct, there was more to come.

Notes

1 Joseph Patrich & Benny Arubas, *A Juglet Containing Balsam Oil (?) From a Cave Near Qumran*, Israel Exploration Journal, Vol. 39, Jerusalem, Israel, 1989, p. 1

2 Talmud, Ker.5b; TJ, Sotah. 8:1:22c

3 *Meam Lo'ez*, translated by R.Aryeh Kaplan, Moznaim Publishing, NY/Jerusalem, 1990, p. 301

4 Ibid, p.299

5 Patrich & Arubas, Israel Exploration Journal, 1989, p.59

6 Nicholas B. Tatro, *Oil Aged 2000 Years Found in Israel*, Associated Press & Seattle Times, February 16th, 1989, Section A2

7 *Meam Lo'ez*, p.298

8 Luria, in his introduction to *The Copper Scroll from the Judean Desert*, Qiryat Sefer LTD, Jerusalem.

Seeing Red

The dig season that followed our success of unearthing the little juglet of Anointing Oil was fraught with disappointments. Many of the volunteers who had become regulars experienced difficulty in returning for the 1989 excavation. It was back to recruiting workers for the dig.

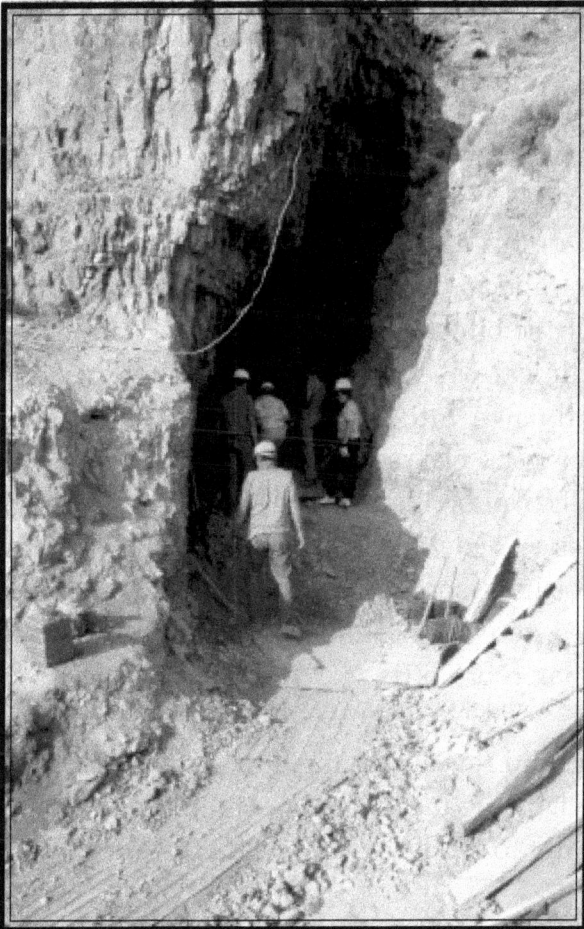

The North Cave, which we dubbed the Spice Cave.

Our shortage was so critical that I had to hire a group of twenty-five Arabs from Bethlehem at one point. There were other disappointments. The number of artifacts being recovered dropped dramatically. But one positive note was that we had finally made our way around the other side of the Cave of the Column, on the north side of the cliffs, facing Jericho. We had done this at the insistence of Zahava who urged me to not ignore the third and fourth lines on the sixth segment of the Copper Scroll:

> *"In the northern opening, dig three cubits. A kalal is there and in it, a scroll."*

With some false starts along the way, our next full dig season kicked off in April of 1992. We were now concentrating all of our efforts in the North Cave. We had twenty volunteers, and as Larry Banks would later note, they were a pretty eclectic bunch, including a court reporter, an airline pilot, a clinical psychologist, a school teacher and housewives all thrown into the mix. Larry would later summarize that we had cleared the cave to bedrock which resulted in the removal of about four hundred tons of rock and soil. There was a real dearth of artifacts in all of this debris, a single Roman potsherd, some cedar wood and burned sticks. Some of the stones were worn, almost polished and could be attributed to human foot traffic.

The chamber did reveal varying degrees of occupation but we were struck by the austere nature of the site, as if there had been an attempt to set the cave aside for the purposes of purity.

"Hey what's this?" Volunteer Glenda Hurst hits 'pay dirt' during the 1992 dig in the North Cave.   Photo credit: Yossi Cohen

That curious state might explainwhat we discovered next. It was an odd, elongated dome formation near the mouth of the cave. We encountered a layer of gravel across the top of the dome, then dirt and after that large stones. The the next layer was more gravel and so on. The rocks were unlike the sharp, broken shards that we found freely in the area caves. It was smooth like the stones found on a river bed. There were eleven alternating levels, each about 45 centimeters thick.

Underneath this feature we found something that baffled the archaeologists on the crew. The last level was parallel to the cave floor. Glenda Hurst, from Goshen Indiana, was brushing a small patch near the dome when she first saw an odd, red substance. She called to Larry Banks, asking him what she had found. No one knew what to make of it.

One thing we did determine right away was that the red material was organic. The test was simple enough. You simply tasted it. Every little grain of the stuff melted in your mouth. Dirt or soil would remain, leaving your tongue gritty. This substance dissolved. It was organic, smelled of cinnamon, and there was over 600 kilos of the stuff!

The Sweet Smell of Success

And the Lord said to Moses, Take to you sweet
spices, storax, and onycha, and galbanum; these
sweet spices with pure frankincense; of each shall
there be a like weight; And you shall make it
a perfume, a confection according to the art of
the apothecary, mixed together, pure and holy;
And you shall beat some of it very small,
and put of it before the Testimony in the Tent of
Meeting, where I will meet with you; it shall be to
you most holy. - Exodus 30:34-38

The initial examination of the puzzling red substance uncovered in the North Cave was done by Dr. Marvin Antelman. If the discovery was composed of cinnamon and other spices, it could prove to be the actual spices used to compound the Holy Incense. A later test by Dr. Terry Hutter, a Palynologist, scrutinized the material's pollen structure.

For something that smells as sweet as incense, it raised a real stink. At the time of his initial analysis of the spices, Dr. Antelman was a paid consultant of the Weizmann Institute in Rehovot, Israel. The good doctor issued his results on that institute's letterhead. When the press arrived, a spokesperson simply stated that Dr. Antelman did not work there, that he was a paid consultant. Critics couldn't dispute his findings, so they complained that the good doctor was (gasp) *merely* a consultant. The disturbing implication here, is that someone who is a consultant lacks the intelligence, or experience, or can not be trusted to deliver the analytical goods.

Those who disparaged his findings never bothered to list any of Dr. Antelman's impressive achievements. If they had taken the trouble, they might have learned that, in addition to authoring two scientific encyclopedias, Antelman is the inventor of Thin Layer Chromatography (Analytical Chemistry, July 1954), a tool utilized internationally for chemical analysis. Dr. Antelman is responsible for hundreds of inventions, including trade secrets and patents on everything from smart card batteries to an EPA-licensed chlorine replacement for swimming pools, which earned him the R&D 100 Award. He's responsible for corrosion-resistant submarine nuclear reactors, life-saving antibiotics, and a cure for AIDS — which won him a nomination for the Nobel Prize. I might also add that Dr. Antelman is an Observant Rabbi, Torah scholar, and a Rabbinic Judge serving on the Council of Scholars of Jerusalem Court and the reconstituted Sanhedrin. In addition, he is a consultant to numerous Fortune 500 companies.

We asked this brilliant man to analyze our discovery because he was able to offer a very special view. As a chemist, he could tell us what we had found; and as a rabbinic scholar, he could determine its place in the codified ritual of Biblical Israel. The red stuff won on both counts. Dr. Antelman ruled out that we had only found dirt, because plain ole soil does not turn to ash when burnt. The pH value of the ashed sample also proved that it was made from plants. This book is not intended for the specialist, I will spare the reader any of the more technical details of the report.[1]

I joined Dr. Marvin Antelman at a news conference at the dig site as he announced his results. He believed we had found the spices used to make the Qetoret.

I was gratified by Dr. Antelman's comments during a press conference, held at the dig site on April 30, 1992, as reported in the Jerusalem Post:

"It passes all of the preliminary tests; bulk density, pH, ash content and reaction with acid you would expect of the pitum haketoret. I'm very excited by this find."[2]

According to Dr. Antleman's initial findings, the red powder was incense used by the priests during Temple services. It is an extraordinary blending of spices, as described in the Torah and the Talmud, from a formula given to Moses by the Creator. The mixture was called *Qetoret*. It is the Hebrew word for an aroma that rises, circles and spreads. The Aramaic root denotes "connection". Both of these meanings convey the power that the Holy Incense has to elevate the mood and the soul of those who experience its heady bouquet.[3]

A detailed formula for compounding the spices is given in the Talmud (*Kritot 6a*) :

Ingredient	Translation	Amount
Tzawri	Balm	70 maneh
Tziporen	Onycha	70 maneh
Khelbona	Galbanum	70 maneh
Levonah	Frankincense	70 maneh
Mohr	Myrrh	16 maneh
Ketzia	Cassia	16 maneh
Shibolet Naird	Spikenard	16 maneh
Kharkom	Saffron	16 maneh
Kosht	Costus	12 maneh
Kilupa	Cinnamon Bark	3 maneh
Kinamon	Cinnamon	9 maneh
Borit Karshina	Karsina Lye	9 kavim
Yain Kafrisin	Cypriot Wine	3 seaim / 3 kavim
Melach Sedomit	Sodom Salt	+ kav
Maaleh Ashan	Smoke Producer	Kol Shehu

The above units of measurement such as *maneh*, *kav* and *seah* are liquid and dry volumetric amounts and we can only estimate their actual values. Interestingly, Dr. Marina Goldman of the Israel Wine Institute at Rehovot stated that the residue of the Cypriot Wine would have given the spices their red color which would have remained even after 2,000 years.[4]

During the 1994 excavation we presented a large sample of the spices to Rav Yehuda Getz, the Chief Rabbi of the Western Wall and the Holy Places in Israel. A sample was also presented to HaRav Ovadia Joseph. Rav Joseph had his own chemist analyze and confirm our findings. Both Rav Joseph and Rav Getz requested that we conduct an experiment and burn some of the incense for scientific purposes.

At their suggestion we combined the spices (*Pitum HaBesamim*) together with the Sodom Salt and the Karshina Lye (the inorganic ingredients stored separately in the cave). Their request was prompted by a concern that the age of the spice might effect the aromatic characteristics of the Qetoret — hence the decision to conduct the experiment.

The final mixture was then burned under the supervision of Rabbi Reuven Grodner, Senior Rabbi at the Hebrew University Department of Judaica and Dr. Terry Hutter, a Palynologist.

The results were astonishing.

Despite the age of the materials used, the aroma was quite unique. Even though the spices had undoubtedly lost some potency, the effect was mesmerizing. The fragrance lingered in the vicinity for several days following the experiment. Several of our volunteers even reported that their hair and clothing retained the aroma. No description could better fit the fragrance than the Biblical passage that refers to the "sweet smelling savor" of the Incense.

Following those tests, Dr. Hutter took a remainder of the spices back to the States to conduct a palynological investigation. His field of study is plant pollens. The fact that we found over 600 kilos of red organic matter, buried in the North Cave, makes it obvious that someone took the trouble to stockpile something that had once been animal or vegetable.

A handful of spices. Our teams eventually collected over 600 kilos from the North Cave.

It was Dr. Hutter's analysis coupled with Dr. Antelman's observations that dispelled any lingering doubts about the exact character of the red substance uncovered that spring day in 1992. Dr. Hutter explained to me that unstable floral elements within the incense should have probably vanished long ago, especially after being buried in a cave for centuries. But, on a microscopic level the actual structure of the plant pollen would remain. Under the microscope Dr. Hutter verified the presence of pollens from nine different plant species, all of which were spices:

Botanical Name	English	Hebrew
Crocus sativus	Saffron	Kharkom
Cinnamomun verum	Cinnamon	Kinnamon
Cinnamomum	Cinnamon Bark	Kilupa
Costus	Cinnamon	Kosht
Commiphoraopobalsanum	Balm	Zori
Commiphora myrrha	Myrrh	Mor
Ferula galbaniflua	Galbanum	Helbonah
Acorus calamus	Cassia	Ketzia
Boswellia carterii	Frankincense	Levonah
Nardostachys jatamansi	Spikenard	Nerd
Styrax officinalis	Onycha	Tziporen

Dr. Hutter identified nine species, but you will note from the above chart, that there are actually eleven ingredients listed. This is because three of the components are various types of cinnamon.

As seen in the chart provided by Dr. Antelman in the opening paragraphs of this chapter, the Talmud details four additional elements not listed above. They are *Karshina Lye, Yain Kafrisen, Melach Sedomit* and *Maaleh Ashan*. They were added as final components just before the mixture was prepared for use, after which the compound was then blessed.

We can glean from all of the Talmudic commentaries that the four additional ingredients were added to make the spices more effective and to increase the volume of smoke.

Karshina Lye was a cleansing agent. The *Yain Kafrisen (Cypress Wine)* was added to strengthen the spices. Exodus 30:35 employs the Hebrew word, *memulach*, which comes from the word *melach* for "salt." This reveals that Sodom Salt was added at some point. Some of the commentaries say this was done because of the commandment to salt the offerings, and it may have been used to purify the mixture.[5]

Maaleh Ashan was called the "smoke raiser," a mysterious element known only to the House of Avtinas. They were the family charged with the responsibility of making the *Qetoret*. This constituent was said to have made the smoke from the incense rise straight as a pillar into the air above the sanctuary.

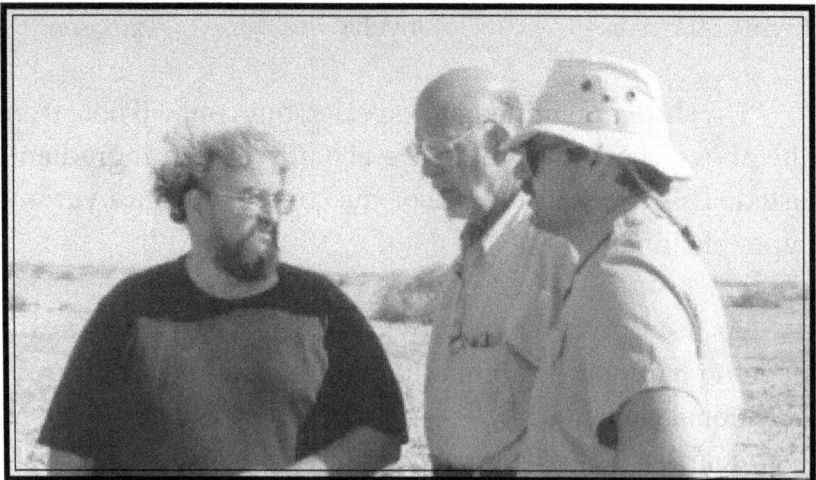

Dr. Terry Hutter (left) and I with volunteer Doug Berner. Terry employed a method known as palynology, which isolated the spices from the pollens, and identified the spices.

It appears that when we opened the North Cave we had stumbled onto an ancient storage site of spices ready for the final processing. When these four elements were mixed with the eleven spices then the blend was ready for use in the Temple. Dr. Hutter conducted another analysis by adding an acid solution to the sample. This catalyst would produce a reaction similar to the spices being added to fire. What followed was what he described as a natural but drastic pH shift. The sample gave off a powerful yet pleasing fragrance. His own recollection of the test should give you an idea the dramatic results:

"The aroma released from the 'spices' during its processing was profuse and almost immediate. It initially saturated my hands as well as the clothes I was wearing. Within a matter of minutes my laboratory and the surroundings (an area of several meters) were affected by the scent released from the 'spices.'"

The intensity of the odor also awakened my dog (a miniature Dachshund) who was asleep in her bed in the lab. On the day of processing, the aroma was so intense that I could almost "taste" it (perhaps this was the original effect during Temple times).

In any case, that evening, upon my return home, the scent that had attached itself on my body and clothes...it was readily apparent to both my wife and daughter.....Within a few weeks the distinct aroma of the spices diminished to a "freshness and cleanness" of the air in my lab and the surrounding area. This aroma was in evidence....for approximately two months. On days of high humidity the aroma would return with greater intensity."[6]

Reading his reaction reminded me of how the Talmud remarks on the remarkable potency of the Qetoret. When it was being used in the Temple in Jerusalem, a bride never needed to wear her perfume, neither did the women down in Jericho. It also caused the goats in Jericho to sneeze.[7]

Dr. Hutter concluded his report by remarking on the purity of the sample, as demonstrated by its state of preservation and the lack of any animal matter. The most exciting aspect of Terry's research is that he was able to isolate and identify all of the spices used to compound *Pitum ha Qetoret*, the Holy Incense as described in Exodus 30:34-5 and Exodus 39:38, as well as the Talmud.

Rabbi Aryeh Kaplan's *Living Torah,* in Exodus Chapter 30, offers an in-depth description of each of the spices. He also translates the traditional Talmudic measurements of weight into pounds and references all other scriptures concerning the *Qetoret.* The Jewish Sages stress the importance of the *Qetoret* and its connection to prayer. The Jewish Prayer Book, known as the *Siddur,* contains many prayers that cite the Qetoret.

Enough of the Holy Incense was compounded for use twice daily during Temple services, in the morning and evening — every day, all year long. In addition, on *Yom Kippur* it was brought into the Holy of Holies. The High Priest filled both of his palms with the *Qetoret,* and tossed it into the fire pan in front of the Ark of the Covenant. A cloud of dense, heady fragrance would twirl upwards in the Holy of Holies and hang in the air just above the Ark.

Notes

1 Dr. Antelman's analysis appears in VJRI's report, *The Copper Scroll and the Excavations at Qumran*, 1995, available from Vendyl Jones Research Institutes, Arlington, Texas, pp.47-49

2 Dell Griffin, "Kumran Dig Shut Down as Chemist Identifies Find", *Jerusalem Post*, May 1, 1992

3 Avraham Sutton, *The Spiritual Significance of the Qetoret*, Yichudim-Silent Unifications, Jerusalem, Israel, 2000, p.12

4 Dr. Antelman's report, p.48

5 *Meam Lo'ez*, translated by R. Aryeh Kaplan, Moznaim Publishers, NY & Jerusalem, 1990, p.313.

6 Dr. Hutter's analysis is also included in the VJRI report, 1995, pp.52-62

7 Talmud, Yoma 39b

God in a Box

"And it shall come to pass, when you multiply and increase in the land, in those days, says the Lord, they shall say no more, 'The ark of the covenant of the Lord.' It shall not come to mind, nor shall they remember it; nor shall they miss it; nor shall that be done any more." - Jeremiah 3:16

Everyone knows where the Ark of the Covenant is — except me. At least that is what I have been told on several occasions. Being viewed as a kind of professional ark hunter brings all kinds of attention, some of it unwanted. As the use of fax machines increased, the ratio of nutty letters to my office increased. They were usually scrawled, never typewritten, in a tightly compacted hand that conveyed the message in a fevered rant.

I am not kidding! These folks have informed me that the Ark of the Covenant was in the Great Pyramid at Giza, because it was the real Mount Sinai. Others whispered that the Ark was in a secret Vatican vault. I have been told that it was in Africa and yes, Arkansas. With the arrival of the internet, the weird letter file actually thinned out. The advent of chat rooms and blog may have given these folks a healthy outlet for their inflamed imaginations. But there is one letter that continues to dog me.

It usually begins, "Jones, the Ark is in Ethiopia..."

Allow me to explain why this particular point of view stirs my blood even more than the nuttier variety. There are grown-ups making a living by milking this misconception in books, badly researched television documentaries and, of course, web sites. I love to study Torah in Hebrew, because the original language possesses a wonderful clarity. But on the subject of the Ark, the English translation offers enough common sense information, that anyone with entry-level comprehension can see that the Ark **cannot** be in Ethiopia.

The Ethiopian tale comes from a legendary text called *Kebra Negast.* Just as in 1 Kings, Solmon and the Queen of Sheba meet — and she is dazzled by him. The Biblical account relates that she returns home. The *Kebra Negast* relates that their meeting produced a son known as Menelik. When he grew up, he went to see Solomon in Jerusalem. The king was taken by this young man that he offered him anything he wanted in the kingdom. He told Solomon he wanted the Ark. When his father refused, Menelik somehow stole the Ark of God from the wisest man in the world.

Not likely.

Solomon had one of the region's best spy networks. He commanded vast armies and a navy. The King would have gone to war to retrieve the Ark. If there is anything to the legend, it may be that a **replica** was given to Menelik.

Several sources relate that the Ark was still in Jerusalem, hundreds of years after Solomon. The Jewish Chronology *Seder Ha Olam* states that King Solomon finished the First

Temple in the year 2932. He passed away in 2964.

When King Hezekiah ruled, he went into the Temple and placed a letter before the Ark. He ruled **two-hundred thirty years after Solomon.** You can read that account in 2 Kings 19:14

II Chronicles, Chapter 35 verse 3, states, "King Josiah said to the Levites, who instructed all Israel, and who had been consecrated to the Lord: 'Put the Ark in the Temple that Solomon had built. It is not to be carried about on your shoulders.'" King Josiah took the throne **three hundred twenty years** after Solomon. In addition, there are numerous Midrash and Talmudic references that tell us the Ark was in the Temple until Jeremiah concealed it.

The aforementioned sources also dispel that notion that Pharaoh Shishak stole the Ark in the time of Rehoboam, as related in 1 Kings 14:25. Rehoboam was the son of Solomon. He took the throne when his father died. If Shishak took the Ark, it certainly would not have been in Jerusalem over three-hundred years later when Josiah ruled (see above). Rabbinic commentaries reveal that Solomon had constructed a special device which employed a system to lower the Ark from the Holy of Holies into a sealed chamber when necessary.

If the Ark had been taken by Shishak, I am convinced that the Bible would have reported such an event. It is certainly not silent when we read the account of the Ark falling into the hands of Israel's enemies, the Philistines. The loss of the ark is detailed in the 4th chapter of 1 Samuel, telling

how it was in the possession of the Philistines for seven
months. There is a fascinating detail from the Oral tradition
that the Ark was stolen during the heat of battle by Goliath.

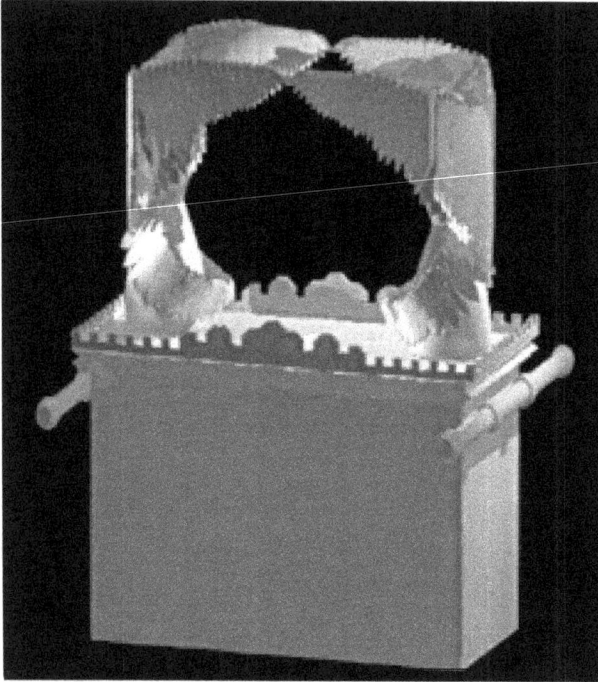

The ark is usually shown with its poles running length
wise. But most commentaries relate that the staves
actually ran along the short sides of the ark.

The Ark was constructed at Mount Sinai while the new
nation of Israel was camped at its base. Though the pattern for
the Ark was given to Moses by the Creator, the task of actually
building it was given to a thirteen-year-old named Betzalel. The
lad's name means "in the shadow of God." He fashioned this
unique instrument which was called the *aron*. The word is

generally translated as chest or coffin. The root of *aron* is *ohr* which means light or energy. It is possible the Ark was able to store and disperse electrical and electromagnetic energy. The description of its design sounds very much like a capacitor, which will hold an electrical discharge before it "arcs" to another source. The Midrash relates that the staves or poles in the Ark were not to lift it, but to actually hold it down. It would cause the priests to "Levi-tate".

The Ark was also said to have pulled massive electrostatic charges from the earth's own electrical fields. One account relates this was the reason that the Ark had to travel so far in advance of the camp — for the safety of the Israelites. When the Ark was in the Holy of Holies, a funnel of fire stood over the *Mishkan* (Tabernacle). There is also a teaching that the Ark caused a kind of temporal displacement.[1]

Uzzah was struck dead after touching the Ark while it was being transported on a wagon (2 Sam.6:7). It could have happened for any number of reasons; after being stolen by the Philistines, it was probably uncovered or Uzzah may not have gone through the purification process. The main reason can be found in Numbers 7:9. The Ark was never to be carried, except on the shoulders of the descendants of Kohath.

There are so many fascinating details about the Ark — enough to fill another book. However, I will close this chapter by addressing the quote from Jeremiah at the start of this section. People often read the 16th verse of Jeremiah, Chapter 3, and believe that there is no use looking for the Ark anymore. Esteemed Jewish sages, such as Rashi, who speak, write, and comprehend the Hebrew language, disagree with the notion that the Ark will never be found again.

Historically, Jeremiah is dealing with those in Judea, whose idea of God had sunk to near idolatry. In their view, as long as the Ark was in still in the Temple, then God was still around. It was as if they thought God was in a box behind the veil in the Holy of Holies. Since He remained there, He surely must approve of their worship and lifestyle. But nothing could be further from the truth.

The Ark was never designed to foster such a corrupt concept. It served many purposes. It represented technology passed along by God Himself. It was also a repository for precious articles such as Torah stones, engraved by the hand of God on pure sapphire; the Rod and the pot of Manna were included. These represented G-d's interaction with mankind in the physical world. More than anything, the Ark was a symbol and never meant to take the place of the Creator.

Jeremiah was telling the people, that in the future, the whole world will worship God in the purest sense. Mankind will fully comprehend that the Creator transcends the constraints of time and space. In essence mankind will not need the Ark to remember the God of Israel.

Notes

1 See *Mysteries of Creation*, Rabbi Dovid Brown, Feldheim Publishers, Nanuet, NY, 1997 pp. 347-350.

Geophysical
or Metaphyscial

Over ten years have passed since discovering the *Qetoret* buried in a shallow rock silo, near the entrance of the North Cave — a site we now refer to as the Spice Cave. Hoping to work smarter, we have attempted to spend less time bent over a shovel and more time employing new technologies that can "see" things that our eyes cannot.

At the start of our 1994-95 excavation season, we secured the services of Alex Beck to drag a clunky high-tech sled across the rock ledges outside the Spice Cave. The device was a transducer used for Ground Penetrating Radar (GPR). This method sends low frequency waves through the various levels of rock, returning signals from the various the strata. It is as impressive as it sounds, except that the data is subject to wide interpretation.

If you have ever squinted at the sonogram of a fetus, you have some idea of the sonic picture scanned by the bouncing waves. At least the latter looks like a child — the GPR image has to be interpreted. In other words, one man's "cavity" is another's "loose fill dirt." We got some very promising readings that revealed, what appeared to be, a massive cavity that lay under the complex of caves scattered around our dig site.

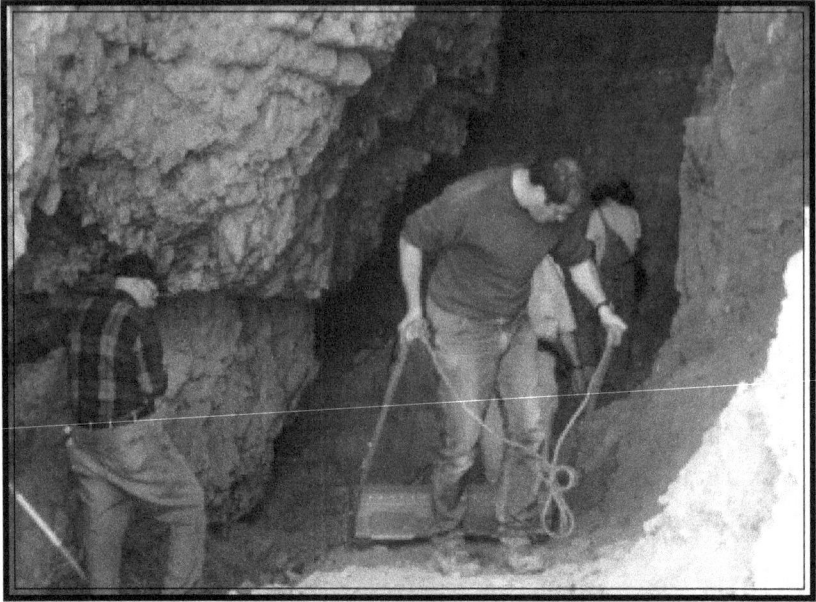

Conducting a geophysical survey of the dig site with Ground Penetrating Radar.

During our last major excavation in 1998, we brought Doron Lipkunsky of Archaeological Engineering Services on board to try out something called Electromagnetic Resistivity Survey (EMR). This method is more elegant and, if done properly, can give you a three-dimensional model of the area surveyed. We put our crew to work hammering little metal probes into the rocky soil about two meters apart, running from inside the Spice Cave and out. Cables were run, laptops were fired up, and a few hours later we had a pretty multi-colored map of the substrata. We were so enthusiastic about the technology we thought it might even show us a box that was concealed somewhere in the depths below us. We didn't see a box, but we did see the depths. Prompted by the images produced from the EMR, we went to work burrowing through the layers of rock, hoping to uncover what lay beneath us.

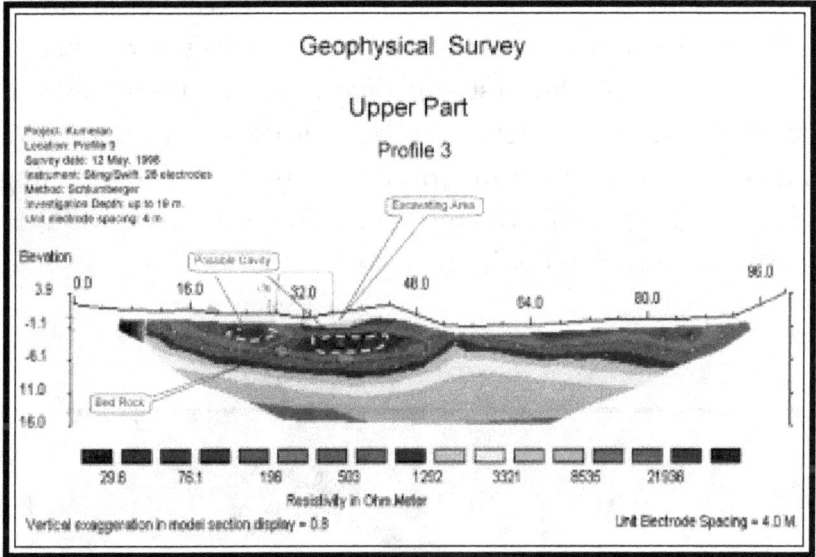

EMR Profile 3 displays two potential cavities below the terrain outside of the Spice Cave near the Cave of the Column.

A number of interesting geological configurations were exposed in the weeks that followed, but no pottery — nothing. A lack of artifacts generally reflects a lack of occupation. We found what looked like manmade domes with alternating layers of various stones. This anomaly was identical to the formation that yielded the 600 kilos of spices from the North Cave above us.

Changes in the governing authority over the area impacted our excavation techniques. Much of region around Qumran was now under the authority of the Nature Preserve,

Israel's version of our Parks and Wildlife Department. Digging in the region these days requires permits from the Israel Antiquities Authority and the Nature Preserve. The latter required us to bag all of the dirt we were excavating. After two months, we had hundreds of bags stacked neatly around the site. Our erstwhile Dig Director and all-around ramrod, Natan Mor, remarked that the dig had turned into a bunker. He joked that the Jordanians were surely watching our progress from across the valley, convinced that we were part of some armed build up.

Our Israeli Dig Director, Natan Mor.

Most of our recent efforts have been confined to mounting more geophysical explorations of the site, and the never-ending task of funding these ventures. Some might criticize my fondness for cutting edge techniques. I embrace the accuracy they offer. As the years go by, and my time grows short, I have become impatient with teacup-and-toothbrush archaeology. During the non-dig seasons, I continue to visit the Cave of the Column during my annual visits to Israel. I have spent many a quiet morning on a rock, overlooking the Dead Sea, contemplating the work still ahead of me.

Between Purim and Passover

Weekly Torah readings, like Jewish Feasts, are movable. It all depends on the cycle of the calendar. If one reads the weekly portion (called a *parsha*) on the first day of January this year, it will not be the same reading on January the first, next year. A Torah *parsha* will often parallel that week's world events. It is not uncommon for an Observant Jew to read the *parsha* that falls on their birthday. Of course, none of this is a surprise to an Observant Jew because they know that the Torah is so much more than the history of the planet and their nation. Torah is also prophecy.

Oddly, I had never thought to look up to the Torah reading the week that the Copper Scroll was discovered— until I was writing this book. I was curious to see if that week's Torah reading might reveal some connection with the discovery of this valuable artifact. What I found was remarkable.

The Copper Scroll cave was found at Qumran on the 14th of March, 1952. The scroll itself was unearthed a few days later on March 20th. The corresponding dates on the Jewish calendar were the 17th of Adar and the 23rd of Adar in the year 5712.

The 14th of March was the Thursday night of Purim. This is the feast that celebrates the Jews victory over their enemies in the Persian Empire. They were saved by their brave Queen Esther from what could have been a Holocaust.

The 16th of March was Shabbat and the Torah reading was *Ki Thissa,* which is Exodus 30:11-34:35. Because it was the first Shabbat after the Purim feast, a special reading known as the *Maftir* was added that week. It was Numbers 19:1-22.

Here, in the Torah reading on the week of the Copper Scroll's discovery, we find a marvelous, uncanny fusion of prophetic words and images that seem to cry out from the past, yet point to the future. *Ki Thissa,* beginning with Exodus 30:11, speaks of collecting **tithes** for the *Mishkan*. A few lines later, a **copper** basin is mentioned as being used by the kohanim to **purify** themselves. Verse 23 then details a list of ingredients for the **Anointing Oil** followed by a command to anoint all of the **holy vessels** for the Mishkan, including the **Ark of the Covenant**. Verse 34 lists all of the **spices** compounded into the *Qetoret,* **the Holy Incense**. The reading also includes the episode of the Golden Calf which is linked to the **Ashes of the Red Cow** and the *parsha* reading ends with a command to engrave a new set of *Luchot* (**Tables of the Law**).

Summing up, the Torah *parsha* for that week of March 20th, 1952 mentions:

- Holy Tithes
- The *Mishkan* (Tabernacle)
- A Copper Basin for Purification
- Anointing Oil
- *Qetoret* (Holy Incense)
- *Luchot* (Tables of the Law)

Masseket Kelim (the text on the Marble Tablets) and *Emek HaMelekh* each list all of the above sacred vessels and both of these sources also state:

> *"These are the holy vessels and the vessels of the Temple that were in Jerusalem and in every place. They were inscribed by Shimur Hu Levi and his companions on a* Luach Nehoshet *(Copper Plate)."*

Additionally, our current translation of the Copper Scroll directly mentions:

- Holy Tithes
- The *Mishkan* (Tabernacle)
- Anointing Oil
- The Purification

Finally, the special *Maftir* included in the Torah reading that same week was Numbers 19:1-2, the statute for preparing:

· The Ashes of the Red Cow
· Water of Purification

The *Hoshen Mishpat* (Jeweled Breastplate), the Vestments of the *Kohen Gadol*, the Rod, the Anointing Oil, the Ashes of the Red Cow, the Ark of the Covenant and the *Mishkan* were all fashioned under the leadership of Moses. Though King Solomon had his own craftsmen assemble precious gold and silver fixtures to fill the First Temple, it still took those irreplaceable hallowed objects created in the Sinai wilderness to fill the Temple of Solomon with holiness. Rabbi Avraham Sutton reminds us that these items were more than ritual instruments; they represented a varying degrees of intimacy with the Creator.[1]

The *Mishkan* and its vessels were fundamental to the very existence of Israel. Though sealed from our sight, every one of the sacred treasures is still intact today, waiting to be recovered. That is exactly why they were hidden, to preserve their holiness for future use in a House of Prayer for All Nations that will be raised up during the Third Commonwealth of Israel.

May it come to pass speedily in our day.

Two Valleys

The Copper Scroll speaks of the desolations of the Valley of Achor. If you visited the region over fifty years ago, you would have found the description very fitting. As you drive down into the Dead Sea Valley from Jerusalem, turn right at the Almog junction, and drive south toward the cliffs. You will drive through the Vale of Achan — or Valley of Achor. We are fairly certain that this region is the ancient Biblical site.

The account in Chapter 7 of the Book of Joshua tells how the Children of Israel arrived in Achor, after the battle of Jericho. It was at this site that Achan was stoned for an act of treason during the siege of the ancient city. His name, literally, meant "trouble".

It is still a wilderness in many respects, but the vigorous Israeli spirit continues to tame the land, reclaiming harsh wastes. The area is now dotted with vineyards and groves of date palms.

There are two Achors before us today. There is the region that I have labored in most of my life, seeking holy treasures. It has been unforgiving in every physical sense. The other Valley of Achor is identical, but is much different in character as described in the prophetic works of Isaiah and Hosea. In both places the connotation is extremely positive, evoking images of security, peacefulness and plenty.

Hosea speaks of vineyards — something that wasn't seen in the region for possibly hundreds of years.

It is possible that we are arriving at a time in history where these particular prophecies are materializing? The same prophet also mentions a mysterious *door of hope* in the Valley of Achor. These prophets speak of the same valley where we have sought to uncover history's greatest treasures. You have read in previous chapters how there was an eighteen-mile tunnel that begins under the Temple Mount and exits in the Valley of Achor.

Could this *door of hope* be the entrance to a vast chamber that holds the sacred Tabernacle and the Ark of the Covenant?

It would be wonderful, and the impact of such a discovery would be incalculable. Consider the effect on the world of finding a beautifully designed, solid gold box that contains two large sapphires (the Torah was written on sapphire). But, I have to consider the alternative.

What if nothing more is found in and around the Cave of Column, and the treasures listed on those deteriorating plates is never recovered?

I have been asked through the years what I would do if these things are not found in my lifetime.

The answer does not trouble me.

As I write these words, I am now seventy-five years old. As a young man I departed my little hometown in the Texas panhandle, hoping I could make a difference in the world. In my efforts to discover how I could have some impact, I managed to collect more truth, heartbreak, joy, adventure, and friendship than any man should expect in one lifetime.

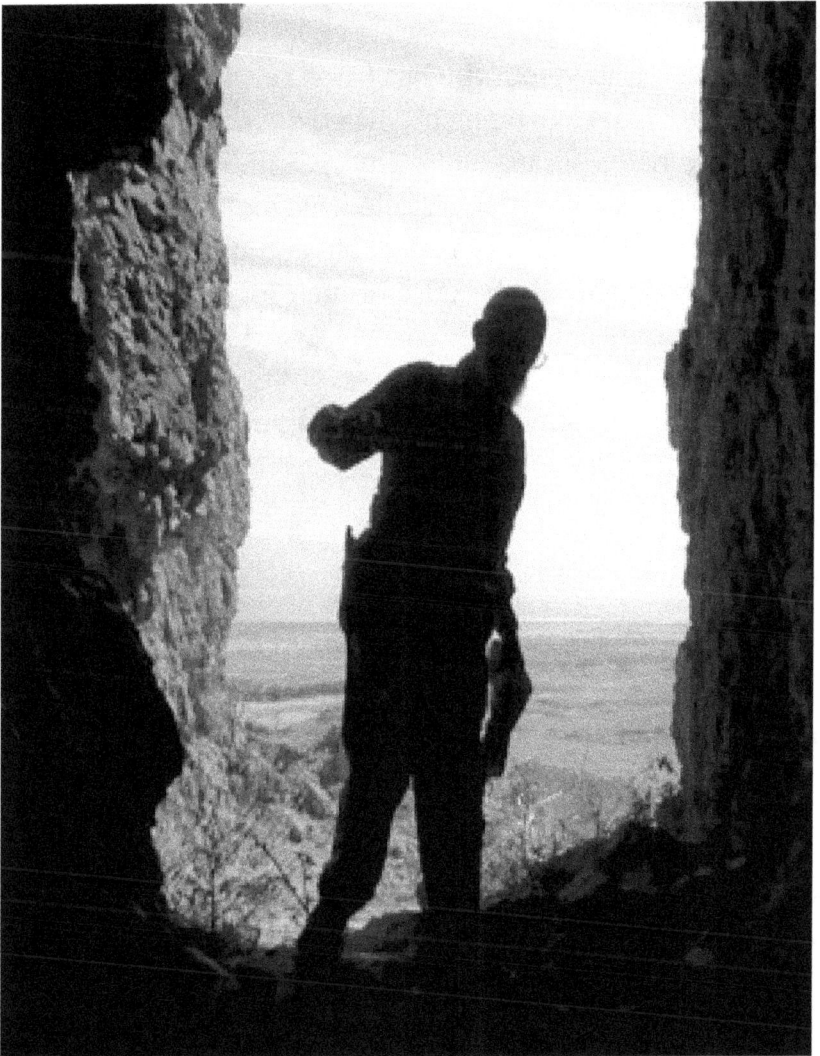

The path that I have trod, in my search for the treasures of
the Copper Scroll, has allowed me to learn from some of the
finest minds driven by the biggest hearts.

Those who have bled, sweated, and cried with me during
the years of digging have made the journey so fulfilling — so
worthwhile.

Maybe I have found what I was seeking. Rabbi Goren
said it best years ago when he visited our dig site. This was a
man who had seen his Holy City reclaimed, and longed to
see the promises for Israel fulfilled. He looked around at the
amazing collection of exhausted, but enthusiastic volunteers
who had come to dig because of their love for G-d and for
the nation of Israel.

"You have found a treasure," Goren said, "the treasure
is you!"

Index

www.ingramcontent.com/pod-product-compliance
Lightning Source LLC
Chambersburg PA
CBHW072122270326
41931CB00010B/1645